London 2012 training guide

Athletics — Field events

First published by Carlton Books Limited 2011
Copyright © 2011 Carlton Books Limited

London 2012 emblem(s) © The London Organising Committee of the Olympic
Games and Paralympic Games Ltd (LOCOG) 2007. London 2012 Pictograms
© LOCOG 2009. All rights reserved.

Carlton Books Limited,
20 Mortimer Street,
London, W1T 3JW

A CIP catalogue record for this book is available from the British Library.
10 9 8 7 6 5 4 3 2 1

ISBN: 978-1-84732-697-3

Printed in China

Editor: Matthew Lowing
Design Direction: Darren Jordan
Design: Fresh Flame
Editorial: Jo Murray and Lesley Levene
Picture Research: Paul Langan
Illustrations: Peter Liddiard
Production: Karin Kolbe

Jason Henderson is Editor of the respected *Athletics Weekly* and has covered
three Olympic Games, three Commonwealth Games and a multitude of European
and World Track and Field Championships for the *Sunday Times*, *The Observer*,
The Times and *The Guardian*. During the 1990s he was a club standard 800 metre
runner with a best of 1:54 and in recent years has run the London Marathon four
times and completed the Hawaii Ironman in 2003.

For my two future Olympians, Leah and Emily

London 2012
training guide

Athletics –
Field events

From beginner to champion

Jason Henderson

CARLTON

Contents

Foreword by Jonathan Edwards, CBE

When I was standing on the podium at Sydney in 2000, with the Olympic Games Triple Jump gold medal around my neck, I started thinking about all the things and people who had made it possible.

There were my coaches, who had spotted my talent and nurtured it; my family, who had supported me as I developed; my determination, which had kept me going when things weren't as positive; and my good fortune with everything.

Winning an Olympic Games gold medal – or any medal in any event, for that matter – isn't easy. It takes incredible hard work and dedication. This *London 2012 Training Guide* won't guarantee you success, but it is an indispensable guide to understanding the events and learning the basics. You need to dedicate yourself to getting fit, and in these pages you will find advice that will prepare you mentally and physically for the challenges ahead.

London 2012 is just around the corner and even if it comes too soon, there is always Rio de Janeiro in 2016. Who knows, you may find yourself standing on the winner's podium, thinking the same thoughts as I did.

Jonathan Edwards, 2011

Introduction

Run! Jump! Throw! Those are the three basic elements of the biggest Olympic Games and Paralympic Games sport – track and field athletics.

Of this trio of physical movements, jumping and throwing make up the section of the sport known as Field

events. Quite simply, there are four jumping and four throwing disciplines: High Jump, Pole Vault, Long Jump and

Triple Jump; and Shot Put, Discus Throw, Hammer Throw and Javelin Throw.

Of course, quite a bit of running is often involved, too. Long jumpers hurtle down the runway before leaping into the sand, while javelin throwers stride forward before launching their javelins into the air. So athletes in field events effectively use all of the three key skills of athleticism.

This means field events are often enjoyed most by the purists – or connoisseurs – of athletics. Simple Running events have greater appeal among the masses, but field events boast a hardcore following of athletics enthusiasts who appreciate not only speed and strength but also technical ability.

In addition, jumping and throwing events have an impressive history to draw on, which adds to their appeal. Events like the Discus, Javelin and Long Jump, for example, date back to the days of ancient Greece.

Athletics field events boast a following of enthusiasts who appreciate not only speed and strength but also technical ability.

Then there are the general health benefits. Learning to jump or vault higher or further, or practising to throw an implement as far as you can, requires a great deal of training. This can be of a technical nature, usually in an athletics arena, or it can involve building fitness in a gym or weights room. Many field event athletes also train their cardiovascular systems – their hearts and lungs – by running or sprinting.

Running or hurdling does not suit everyone's body type. So heavily built athletes might be far better suited to throwing events. Unusually tall and slim athletes, on the other hand, might discover that they excel in the High Jump.

Field events are ideal for young athletes to use as a foundation for their future sporting life. After all, the basic elements of athleticism are at the root of almost every sport. So if you decide to move into football, cricket or rugby in later life, for example, then you will have already learned the basic movements of how to jump and throw.

For older people looking for a challenge and a way to keep fit, field events can also be a great idea. Among other things, they help maintain flexibility and strength – two of the main physical elements that disappear with age.

Together with the physical benefits, there is also a strong social element in athletics. If you join a club you will discover other people with the same goals. Regular group training sessions can enhance your lifestyle, while competitions can liven up otherwise dull weekends.

The basics

To jump or throw to your maximum
potential, you first need to become a
student of the sport. So this chapter
offers some background and history on
the disciplines you are about to tackle.

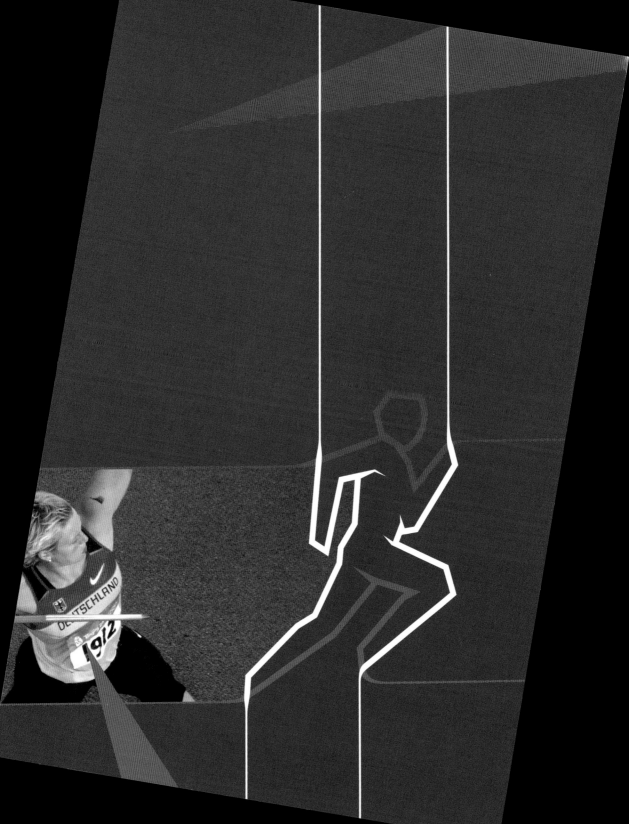

Field events

When track and field is mentioned as a sport, the field part always comes second. Yet given the huge impact Field events have had on the Olympic Games, this is rather unfair, and here we explain why these sports are so important.

Athletics is arguably the most competitive sport on the planet. More than 200 nations compete in Olympic or world competitions. The elite athletes who compete in the international arena are also the best of the best. Almost all children have the opportunity to run, jump or throw when they are at school, and the best of the best end up as elite athletes who compete at international level. Compared to sports such as rugby, cricket, baseball and American football, which are only played by a limited number of countries, athletics is a truly global sport.

Field events are a huge part of this. Of the 47 track and field medal events on the Olympic programme for men and women, 16 of them are jumping or throwing events. This does not include the Heptathlon or Decathlon either, both of which include a number of jumps and throws.

Field events are sometimes not as highly regarded as the more glamorous track events of sprints, hurdles and middle and long distance running. Yet field events have produced some of the most iconic moments in Olympic

Men

Event	World Record	2008 Olympic Champion
High Jump	2.45m Javier Sotomayor (Cuba) 1993	2.36m Andrey Silnov (Russia)
Pole Vault	6.14m Sergey Bubka (Ukraine) 1994	5.96m Steve Hooker (Australia)
Long Jump	8.95m Mike Powell (USA) 1991	8.34m Irving Saladino (Panama)
Triple Jump	18.29m Jonathan Edwards (Great Britain) 1995	17.67m Nelson Evora (Portugal)
Shot Put	23.12m Randy Barnes (USA) 1990	21.51m Tomas Majewski (Poland)
Discus Throw	74.08m Jurgen Schult (East Germany) 1986	68.82m Gerd Kanter (Estonia)
Hammer Throw	86.74m Yuriy Sedykh (Soviet Union) 1986	82.02m Primoz Kozmus (Slovenia)
Javelin Throw	98.48m Jan Zelezny (Czech Republic) 1996	90.57m Andreas Thorkildsen (Norway)

history from some of the world's most famous athletes.

Legends Carl Lewis and Jesse Owens of the United States were not only superb sprinters but also world record-breaking long jumpers. Fanny Blankers-Koen, the Dutch star of the London 1948 Games, excelled in High Jump and Long Jump, together with sprints. American thrower Al Oerter stamped his name on Olympic history by winning four Discus titles from 1956 to 1968.

The field events are listed in the table below, together with the reigning Olympic champions and current world record-holders for men and women.

Athletics is a truly global sport and 16 of its 47 medal events are field events.

Women

Event	World Record	2008 Olympic Champion
High Jump	2.09m Stefka Kostadinova (Bulgaria) 1987	2.05m Tia Hellebaut (Belgium)
Pole Vault	5.06m Yelena Isinbayeva (Russia) 2009	5.05m Yelena Isinbayeva (Russia)
Long Jump	7.52m Galina Chistyakova (Soviet Union) 1988	7.04m Maurren Maggi (Brazil)
Triple Jump	15.50m Inessa Kravets (Ukraine) 1995	15.39m Françoise Mbango (Cameroon)
Shot Put	22.63m Natalya Lisovskaya (Soviet Union) 1987	20.56m Valeri Vili (New Zealand)
Discus Throw	76.80m Gabriele Reinsch (East Germany) 1988	64.74m Stephanie Brown-Trafton (USA)
Hammer Throw	78.30m Anita Wlodarczyk (Poland) 2010	76.31m Aksana Miankova (Belarus)
Javelin Throw	72.28m Barbora Spotakova (Czech Republic) 2008	71.42m Barbora Spotakova (Czech Republic)

A brief history

Many field events boast a rich tradition dating back several centuries – and in some cases thousands of years. The events, however, have evolved greatly since their original days and have undergone many changes.

Origins

The origin of many field events can be traced back to the days of Ancient Greece and around 776 BC. Indeed, the blue riband event of the early Olympic Games was the Pentathlon, which featured Wrestling, sprinting (called the 'stadion'), Long Jump, Javelin and Discus.

Most people today are familiar with images of sculptures that depict Greek athletes throwing the discus. The javelin, meanwhile, was popular due to the fact it was one of the main weapons of that era.

In addition to spears, stones were also thrown during hunting or warfare – and this evolved into what we know today as the Shot Put. The background of the Pole Vault, on the other hand, began when men used to clear streams and ditches using long sticks.

When it came to the Long Jump, there was a slight twist on the modern-day event, as Greeks often used 'halteres', or small hand weights, which they used to propel themselves to greater distances as their bodies flew threw the air.

Early Competitions

The Tailteann Games of ancient Ireland were an important landmark in the history of the sport – they are thought to precede even the Ancient Greek Games by a century or more. Athletics was then kept alive during the Middle Ages, most spectacularly in Scotland, where the Highland Games are thought to date back to the 14th century or earlier.

Dick Fosbury

If ever there was a sportsman who changed the nature of his event, it is Dick Fosbury. The American high jumper captured the imagination of the world when he won gold at the Mexico 1968 Olympic Games using an unusual 'flop' – a technique that is now used by almost every top-level jumper. Initially, Fosbury used the scissors technique, but he felt he could improve by lowering his centre of gravity by sprinting diagonally at the bar and going over head first on his back.

He dazzled his rivals with a clearance of 2.24 metres and, in the space of one competition, the Fosbury Flop became all the rage.

The sport really began to establish itself in the 18th and 19th centuries, though, and although pedestrianism – or long-distance running and walking challenges – dominated, there was also the gradual development of the traditional track and field events that we see today.

Oxbridge students, for instance, took part in formal athletics competitions during the 1860s, with High Jump and Long Jump on the programme.

Modern Developments
The culmination of this was the first modern Athens 1896 Olympic Games . Here, six of the modern-day field events were featured, although subsequent Games at the turn of the 20th century saw several tweaks to the rules that we know today, with medals awarded for, among other things, standing Long Jump, High Jump and Triple Jump competitions, plus Javelin and Discus throws.

With the technique for various events in its infancy, not surprisingly the first few decades of the 20th century saw various methods being used until certain ones began to gain more credibility and became accepted as the norm.

Once in a while, though, an incredible event would occur that would rewrite the history of an event. Dick Fosbury and his 'flop' High Jump technique in the 1960s was one such example of that.

The standing Long Jump last appeared at the Stockholm 1912 Olympic Games.

Developments in Field events

Developments in equipment and technique – the latter often inspired by exceptional individual athletes – and also coaching and training methods have led to a gradual improvement in field event standards during the past century.

The past 100 years have seen an ironing out of the technical confusion and uncertainty that reigned during early Olympic Games. Today, most athletes know what the best method of achieving their best jump or throw is, but it has taken years of trial and error to reach this point.

Jumping Events

In the High Jump, a variety of techniques fought for prominence in the first half of the 20th century. Among them were the scissors, Western roll and straddle, and the Eastern cut-off. But the key development was Dick Fosbury introducing his 'flop' technique to win gold at the Mexico 1968 Olympic Games (see page 12). Many others followed his lead – and it was made all the easier by the introduction of softer landing mats during this period.

In the Pole Vault, apart from early contests being judged by distance and not height, and athletes landing on sawdust and not a soft mat, the primary developments in this event have been in the type of pole used. Pioneers in the mid-19th century used heavy ash or cedar poles with iron spikes in the base. Soon after, bamboo was used, followed by steel and aluminium. Eventually, more flexible fibreglass or carbon fibre poles were developed, with world records climbing steadily as the equipment improved.

In the Long Jump, a variety of techniques continue to be used. The most notable landmarks, though, are the extraordinary breakthrough distances achieved by

Bob Beamon

'Beamonesque' is a word that has spread beyond athletics and is used to describe an extraordinary, ground-breaking performance in any sport.

Its origins come from the exploits of long jumper Bob Beamon, who leapt 8.90m at the Mexico 1968 Olympic Games. The 22-year-old New Yorker was far from being the favourite for gold, but he smashed the 1967 world record by 55 centimetres. Amazingly, the world record had only improved by 19cm in the 33 years since another legend, Jesse Owens, broke the world record in 1935.

When told of his achievement, Beamon was so overcome with emotion that he collapsed in shock.

American athletes Jesse Owens in 1935 and Bob Beamon in 1968 – both records stood for many years.

The main changes in the Triple Jump, meanwhile, have included alterations to the sequence of hops or jumps taken during the attempt. It has also benefited from improvements in coaching, training methods and equipment – such as superior runway surfaces and landing areas – as have all the Field events.

The Triple Jump has only recently been contested by women in major events, as has the Hammer.

Throwing Events

The flight of the javelin has been dependent on technology. For example, a redesign to the implement was made in 1986 after the world record set in 1984 reached a dangerous distance of 104.8 metres and many throws were also landing 'flat' (see page 110). Since then, the record distance thrown has been less than 100m.

In the Shot Put, two main techniques continue to be used – the glide and the spin, which was used by world record-holder Randy Barnes in 1990.

The Hammer features a ball at the end of a wire; this was not always the case, however. The ball has often sat at the end of a stick, as it continues to do today in the Highland Games.

Refined techniques and technological advances have helped athletes reach new heights and distances.

The athletics arena

With many events often taking place at the same time in a relatively small arena, track and field athletics is a busy spectacle. Given this, each event is placed in the best possible position to ensure safety and enjoyment.

The early modern Olympic Games were held in unusual arenas such as the Panathinaiko Stadium, which staged the Athens 1896 Games and was 333.33 metres long. Soon after, the size and shape of track and field stadium became more standard and cinder or ash tracks were replaced by the all-weather synthetic surfaces that we see today.

Field events largely take place within the 400m six- or eight-lane tracks that now dominate the sport. The Long Jump and Triple Jump runways are 40m long with a sandpit for athletes to land in at each end. The Pole Vault runway is the same length, with a box at the end for planting the pole and a mat to land on. Depending on the arena, these runways can sometimes sit just outside the running track lanes.

The High Jump area is situated at one of the bends and is an arc area, giving athletes enough room to run at the bar and then land on a large mat.

The four throwing events typically begin on one side of the stadium. The Discus Throw and Hammer Throw athletes start their event in a large metal cage that sits at one of the corners of the arena. The Shot Put circle is placed at the other corner of the arena nearest the throwing cage. The Javelin Throw runway is in an area that is central and parallel to the straights of the running track.

These throwing positions are all designed to allow the implements to land in the middle of the entire arena and therefore minimise the chances of injuries to nearby track and field athletes.

It results in an action-packed sight, with several competitions taking place

Long and triple jumpers enjoy a run-up that is adjacent to the running itself.

Hammer throwers can reach distances of 60–80 metres so safety is paramount.

Electronic scoreboards relay the athlete's performance to the stadium spectators.

simultaneously – usually in key positions right next to large groups of spectators – and this is why the athletics arena is often regarded as the heart of the Olympic Games.

During winter, indoor competitions are also popular and feature High Jump, Pole Vault, Long Jump, Triple Jump and Shot Put competitions within a stadium that houses a track of just 200m.

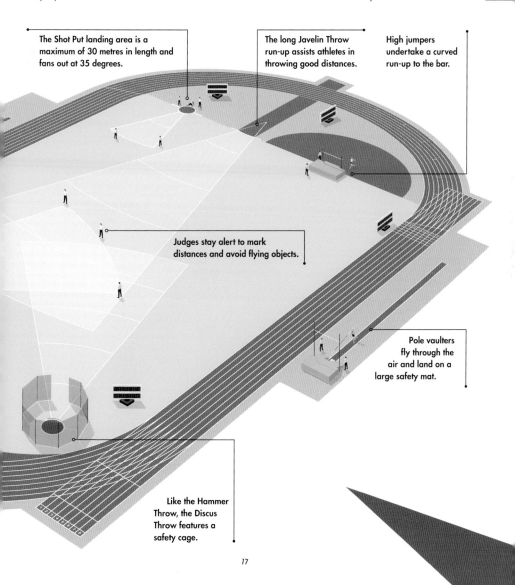

The Shot Put landing area is a maximum of 30 metres in length and fans out at 35 degrees.

The long Javelin Throw run-up assists athletes in throwing good distances.

High jumpers undertake a curved run-up to the bar.

Judges stay alert to mark distances and avoid flying objects.

Pole vaulters fly through the air and land on a large safety mat.

Like the Hammer Throw, the Discus Throw features a safety cage.

General rules and measurements

Here is a simple event-by-event guide to the basic rules behind the jumping and throwing disciplines, including how efforts are measured, how many attempts you can take and how you can win.

General Rules

There are a number of standard rules that apply across several Field events. For example, throwers must start from a stationary position and stay in the throwing area until their implements have landed and then retreat from the back of the Throwing area. The implements must also stay within the sector lines after they have been thrown.

There are three to six attempts for all the throws and horizontal jumps, depending on the type of competition – and the best result counts.

A good understanding of field events rules is essential to success.

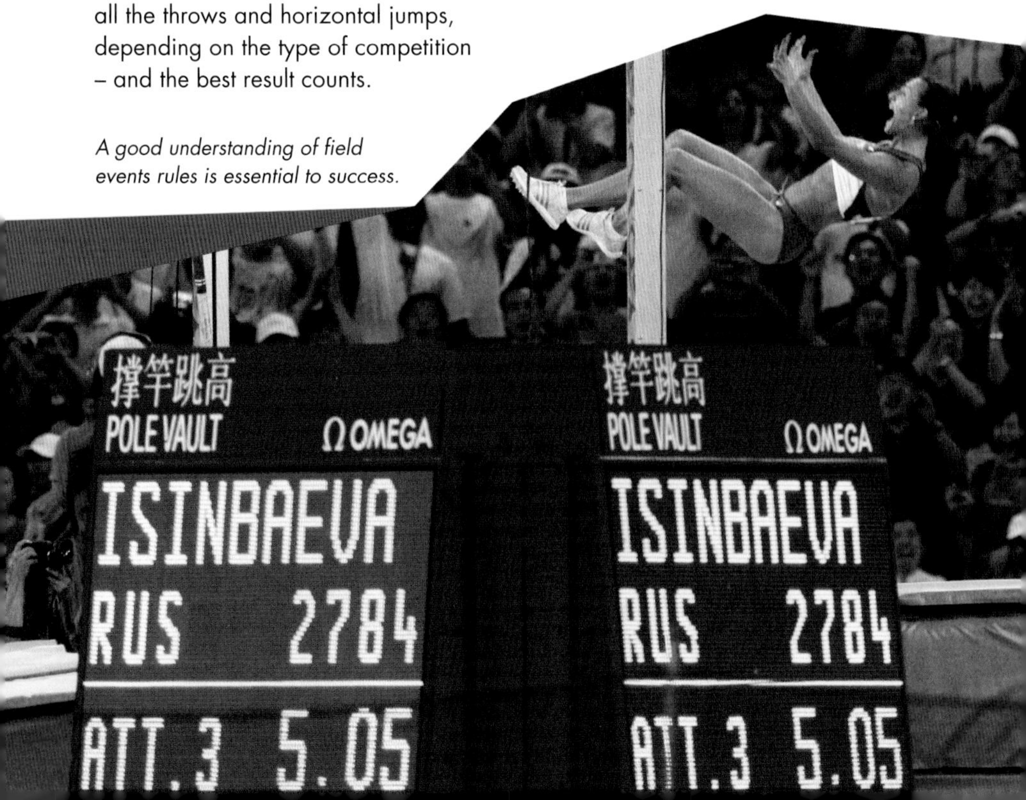

How Events are Measured

All jumps and throws are measured using the metric system.

For throws, distances are measured from the mark made by the implement on landing or the place where the judge saw it land – whichever is nearest to the area from where it was thrown.

Throws are also measured to the nearest centimetre below the reading on the tape or automatic measuring device.

撑竿跳高
POLE VAULT   Ω OMEGA

ISINBAEVA
RUS   2784

ATT.3 5.05

撑竿跳高
POLE VAULT   Ω OMEGA

ISINBAEVA
RUS   2784

ATT.3 5.05

A wind gauge is used for Long Jump and Triple Jump, with records disallowed if the speed of the tailwind is greater than 2 metres per second. And in these two horizontal jumps, the distance measured is from the mark in the sand nearest to the take-off board.

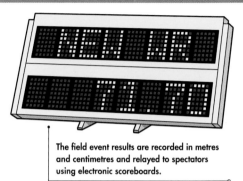

The field event results are recorded in metres and centimetres and relayed to spectators using electronic scoreboards.

High Jump

As the height of the bar is gradually raised by 5cm, 3cm or 2cm increments during the competition, athletes continue to jump until they have had three successive failures (which may be at different heights).

Pole Vault

As in High Jump, athletes continue until they have three successive failures. Vaulters must also not go above the grip taken by their upper hand after take-off.

Long Jump

Athletes must leap from behind the leading edge of the take-off board, which often has Plasticine on it to help judges decide if an attempt was a foul or not.

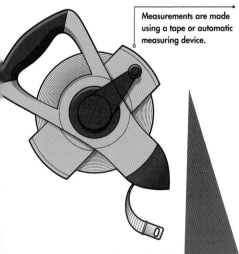

Measurements are made using a tape or automatic measuring device.

Triple Jump

Similar to the Long Jump and the athlete must follow the simple but strict 'hop, step and jump' sequence.

Shot Put

The shot must be pushed and therefore remain in close contact to the neck at the start and not brought back behind the shoulder line.

Discus Throw

In this event, throwers can use chalk to improve their grip, but not gloves.

Hammer Throw

If the hammer head hits the ground before or during a throw and no infringements have taken place, the thrower can stop and try again. If the hammer hits the cage but still lands within the sector lines, the throw is valid.

Javelin Throw

Athletes must not tread on – or outside – the arc line. The javelin must be thrown from above the shoulder and the point must touch the ground first.

General training

Before you compete, there is plenty of preparation that must be done first. Here we look at the basics of training: how to keep safe, what to wear, what to eat, plus psychology, setting targets and the all-important warm-up.

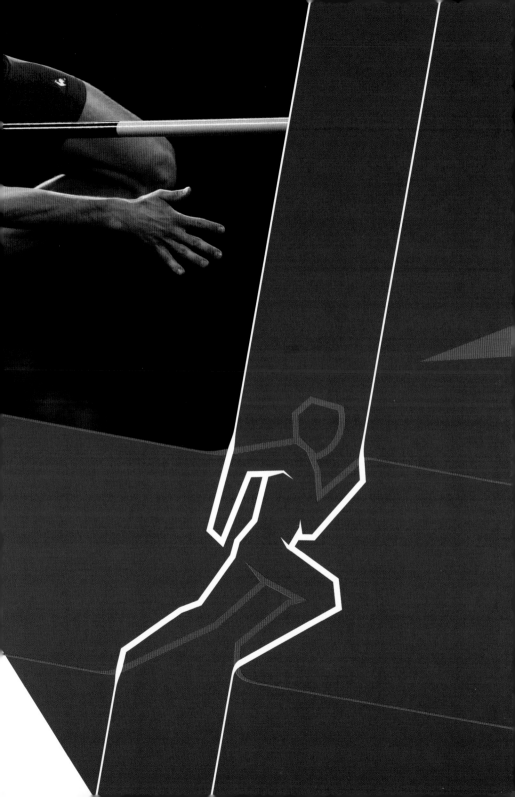

Getting started

If you are ready to lace up your training shoes, but not quite sure where to start, here is some simple background on training, plus some crucial advice on signing up with a club and coach.

Join Up!

One of the golden rules when taking up athletics is to join a club. This is especially important if you are planning to take part in one of the technical field disciplines.

At an athletics club you will find coaches who specialise in various track and field events and other athletes to train with. This is vital, as a good coach will explain the intricacies of the event or events, answer any questions you have and squeeze the most out of your potential.

They will have the experience that you are missing and be able to offer an objective view on your ability and technique after watching you in action.

What's in Store

When it comes to training, there are many different elements involved. Lots of the training principles are similar across the board, too, despite the eight field events being very different from each other.

The key elements are:

- **Speed** – This can be developed by fast running, drills and training techniques such as hill sprints.
- **Strength and power** – Strength is forged in the gym and weights room, mainly by lifting moderate to heavy weights. Power is the ability

to maximise strength at the fastest possible rate and is developed by weightlifting or bounding drills.

- **Flexibility** – The more mobile you are, the better you will be able to jump and throw. Stretching and mobility exercises will improve this.
- **Technique** – Brute strength and demon speed will only get you so far. Smooth and effective technique is vital if you want to fulfil your potential.

Speed, strength and flexibility are important field athlete characteristics but good technique is essential.

And That's Not All

In addition, general fitness and endurance are important. Increases in fitness and stamina will allow you to complete more specific strength or technical training. This kind of work is often carried out in the winter, or off-season, too, with more event-specific technical training done in the pre-season and competitive periods.

As for differences between jumps and throws training, the jumping events generally require more speed and training drills, whereas throwing events demand a greater emphasis on strength, with more hours subsequently spent in the weights room. Very generally, jumps training focuses heavily on the legs, while throwers will work on their upper bodies a little more.

None of the disciplines can ever shirk on technical training, though. Mastering the skill of each event is perhaps the most important aspect of all.

Training safety

Throwing implements are derived from weapons of warfare, so extreme care should be taken when using them in an athletics environment. Jumping, too, can be a risky business. Given this, safety is paramount.

Before you even step into an athletics arena, if you are an adult who has not done regular fitness training for several years then visit your doctor first to have a health check.

Youngsters should also be careful, as a mixture of inexperience and lack of physical strength is a recipe for disaster.

In the Gym
Accidents can easily happen in the weights room or gym. Make sure you train with a partner or ensure you are overseen by a coach.

Do not lift heavy equipment unless you have already had some previous instruction. Together with this, training partners or coaches who act as 'spotters' are invaluable. If you get into trouble with equipment, they will be on hand to rescue you.

Role of the Coach
A good coach can reduce the risk of accidents and injuries by offering solid instruction to athletes. In addition, the coach should steer athletes to follow a sensible progression of skills, as incorrect or poor technique can lead to injury.

The coach should also warn athletes to be on their guard in a dangerous environment such as the gym – and especially the athletics arena itself on a training or competition day. Teaching awareness and responsibility to athletes is an important part of coaching; in turn, experienced athletes will hopefully pass these lessons on to those just starting.

Finally, the club and coach should ensure that equipment is well maintained. Safe equipment in an event like the Pole Vault, for example, is vital.

In the Arena
The throwing implements – the javelin, discus, hammer and shot – are potentially very dangerous due to their shape and size. Accidents in athletics are very rare, but only because strict safety guidelines are followed. For these, always seek guidance from a coach or other senior member of an athletics club.

Extreme caution should be taken at all times. Use your eyes and also your ears – in the UK, a horn is sounded when a throw is about to be made.

Use common sense by not wandering into the

The athletics arena has the potential to be a dangerous environment and extreme caution should be taken at all times.

in-field where throwing implements land. Do not walk or run across lanes or runways either – athletes have been knocked unconscious or badly injured by other runners when they have not looked where they are going.

For more advice on safety in your chosen event, see the individual discipline pages.

Training clothing and equipment

There are no prizes for appearance, but wearing the correct type of shoes and clothing will definitely help improve your performance. In addition, there is a plethora of optional gear and gadgets that you can add to your athletics kit bag.

Anyone with shoes, shorts and a T-shirt can run. Field events are more complicated, though, with lots of equipment required to complete the events. However, it need not be too overwhelming – like running, the main requirements are footwear and basic clothing.

Shoes

If you are serious about your sport, there are specialist spikes or shoes for each of the field events – these are described in more detail in the individual discipline pages later in the book. For now, be aware that Javelin and Triple Jump spikes are very different from standard running spikes. Triple Jump spikes, for example, feature more cushioning due to the bounding involved in the event. A special type of shoe is needed to glide or spin around the throwing circles, too.

Clothing

If you have joined a club, then you will already have a brand-new vest in your local colours. If temperatures are chilly, though, keep warm by wearing a T-shirt or long-sleeved top underneath it. A decent tracksuit and, ideally, water- or shower-proof gear will complement it well – your body will not perform at its best if your muscles are cold.

Kit Bag

To carry all your gear, a good kit bag is essential. There are many small items that can be added to the kit bag. Safety pins to put your competition number on, for instance.

Equipment

When it comes to throwing implements, athletes can use their own instead of those supplied by organisers. They must be checked and approved first, however.

Pole Vault athletes also have their own poles, which is not surprising as they are highly personalised items of equipment. Poles are graded according to the load that will bend them, so they are designed to match vaulters of a certain size and weight. Poles can also be of any length or weight, but the surface must be smooth and a binding of no more than two layers of tape is allowed.

Gym and weights equipment is also important. Much of this is readily available in public gyms, although some athletes prefer to use their own equipment at home.

Linked to this, specialist weightlifting shoes and a belt to support the lower back are recommended for athletes spending a lot of time pumping iron.

Gloves are also useful when it comes to weights work. Hammer throwers can use gloves, too, when they throw.

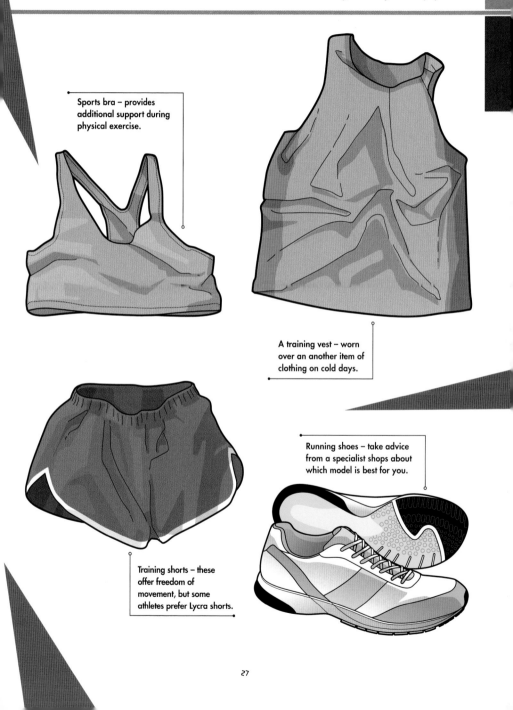

Sports bra – provides additional support during physical exercise.

A training vest – worn over an another item of clothing on cold days.

Running shoes – take advice from a specialist shops about which model is best for you.

Training shorts – these offer freedom of movement, but some athletes prefer Lycra shorts.

What do you want to achieve?

If you want to win a medal at the Olympic Games or simply achieve a personal best performance, you have far more chance of reaching your goal if you figure out a smart training programme.

An athlete who trains the same remains the same. One of the main principles of training is to increase the workload steadily so that you enjoy gradual gains – and this can be achieved by setting targets.

This is best done by sitting down with your coach and working out what you want to achieve and how long it might take to get there. The targets should be realistic but challenging. If you reach for the stars then the least that will happen is that you will hit your head on the ceiling.

Keeping a diary and training plan is a great way to start and planning can be split into weekly, monthly and annual sections. More long-term (three- or five-yearly) plans are not a bad idea either.

When putting together your schedule, consider all the sessions available to work on various factors such as strength, speed, fitness and technique. You will need to work on your weaknesses and not ignore your strengths – and the training schedule will also vary according to what time of year it is.

Above all, ask yourself what you want to achieve. It might be winning a medal at a national or regional age-group championship, for example, or throwing or jumping a certain distance or height – or perhaps both. And then, when you have decided what your goals are, work out how you can best get there.

In addition to sessions at the track or in the gym, you can monitor your weight and sleep patterns. Then, if you enjoy a successful competition, you can look back to see what worked.

Remember, if you fail to plan, you are effectively planning to fail.

A diary and training plan are excellent tools for fulfilling your potential.

Planning your schedules

- **Weekly** – This is all about structuring your daily programme so that your training sessions weave around your other commitments. Improvements in performance will come from consistent training, so having a regular weekly programme that you can stick to will be a big help.
- **Monthly** – Here you can plan competitions you might do and also set goals, such as lifting a certain weight on a particular exercise in the gym or focusing on a particular part of your technique. You might also include in your programme harder and easier weeks.
- **Annual** – Planning yearly goals is vital. And beyond this you can set a long-term plan with a series of annual targets.

Fitness training

Before you focus on the technical aspects of jumping and throwing events, it is sensible to work on your general fitness. Improve this and you will ultimately be able to jump and throw higher and further.

The Importance of Practice

Success in athletics does not come overnight and it will take several years of training for you to reach your potential. Studies, in fact, have shown that it requires around 10,000 hours' worth of practice – or two to three hours every day for a decade – to become proficient at a field event.

Given this, there is perhaps some truth in the mythical story of Milo of Croton. One of the stars of the Ancient Greek Olympic Games, Milo was famed for being able to lift a four-year-old bull on his shoulders. And according to legend he achieved this great strength by starting with a new-born ox and lifting it every day until it was fully grown.

This theory of gradual progression over many years works perfectly in athletics and during the early stages of your training for field events you will look to focus on general fitness. Because the stronger and fitter you become, the more quality technical work you will be able to handle at a later stage.

Getting Fit

Running is a perfect way to get fit and is especially appropriate for jumpers and Javelin throwers. Shot Put, Discus and Hammer athletes will usually be more heavily built, though, and might prefer to fine-tune the aerobic system by biking, swimming or rowing.

It is important for beginners – or athletes starting their preparation period after a long break – to spend time on 'conditioning' training, too. This means strengthening and stretching every part of the body so that it can withstand the rigours of the more specific training that will come at a later stage.

Circuit training is an ideal way to achieve this. Lifting high repetitions of light weights is also good. Plyometrics – or bounding exercises – are ideal, but at a gentle pace to begin with. And don't forget to incorporate plenty of stretching and flexibility.

In improving your general fitness, you will ultimately be able to jump and throw higher and further.

Simple fitness exercises

- **Press-up** – A popular exercise with enduring appeal for the simple reason that almost your entire body has to work to do it.
- **Sit-up** – Strong abdomen muscles are vital, whatever field event you do.
- **The Plank** – Again, this exercise works most muscles in the body, especially your core. Lie face down, resting on your forearms and toes, and hold for as long as you can.

Intensive training

To jump or throw to your absolute potential, you must be prepared to train hard. Here we look at what it takes to be the best you can.

General fitness training will turn you into a better athlete, but more specific training will make you a better jumper or thrower.

While beginners might train three or four times a week, more experienced and serious athletes will train almost every day. The really committed athletes, meanwhile, will gradually – over months and years – build up to about 10–12 sessions a week.

Athletics can be fun, but it is also hard work and success does not come easily. It is hugely challenging. Given this, many gruelling hours are spent in the gym, weights room and on the track. Jumpers and vaulters spend hours perfecting their run-ups to take-off. Throwers work on delivering their implement into the air as powerfully and flawlessly as possible.

As well as gym, weights and technical training, serious athletes carry out endless drills in order to improve their form – or style – and also to help injury-proof their bodies.

It is not only distance runners who go to altitude in order to improve their endurance by boosting their red blood cell count by training in the thin air. Jumpers and throwers do this as well, with javelin throwers Jan Zelezny and Steve Backley pioneered altitude training in the 1980s.

Athletics training is a 24/7 job and outside the actual training sessions ice baths, massage and physiotherapy are also daily occurrences in order to speed recovery between sessions.

Finally, lots of work is carried out in front of computer screens. Coaches and athletes analyse their technique using slow-motion video footage. The annual training schedule is also constantly updated, with a different emphasis at various times of the year. This is designed to allow athletes to reach a peak when they need to and is called 'periodisation'.

To achieve your potential, you must be prepared to train hard.

How the professionals train

High jumper Martyn Bernard and long jumper Greg Rutherford are two British athletes who train together at a UK Athletics High Performance Centre in Lee Valley in London under the same coach, Dan Pfaff.

To athletes like Bernard and Rutherford, athletics is a full-time job and they spend several hours each day working on their fitness and technique. At Lee Valley, they have great facilities, training partners and support staff, such as physiotherapists, all under the same roof.

Diet and hydration

Jumpers and throwers have different dietary demands compared with sprinters, hurdlers and runners. Nutrition before training and competition will also vary.

Healthy Eating

Primarily power athletes, jumpers and throwers need to eat enough carbohydrates to fuel training sessions, although carbohydrate requirements do not reach the same high levels as for runners – field athletes do not suffer from glycogen depletion or hit 'the wall'. It is important, though, to eat a good balance of carbohydrates, fats and proteins, with plenty of fruit and vegetables to maintain

A winning diet will lead to better performances.

healthy levels of vitamins and minerals.

One simple rule of nutrition is to eat fresh food and avoid, where possible, over-processed foods.

When choosing carbohydrates, pick those with a low glycaemic index (GI). These types, such as whole-grain breads and pasta, break down more slowly, releasing glucose gradually into the bloodstream. Eating low-GI foods will effectively fatigue-proof your body.

Maximising the body's power-to-weight ratio is also important, especially for jumpers and javelin throwers. Shot, discus and hammer throwers can afford to be slightly heavier, as the athlete's weight can contribute to a greater throw. But jumpers and javelin throwers need to retain low body-fat levels while being strong and muscular.

To achieve this requires an eating strategy that will enable a maintenance or increase of the muscle mass, coupled with the lowest possible body-fat percentage.

Ideally, power athletes should have a protein intake of between 1.2 and 2 grams per kilogram of body weight, with the lower value for athletes who are trying to sustain muscle mass and the higher value for athletes who want to increase muscle mass.

Fluid Intake

Allied to good nutrition, hydration is vital. Water makes up two-thirds of our body weight, so liquid levels need to be topped up in order to maintain performance levels. Typically, an athlete should drink 1.2 litres (six to eight glasses) of water each day. In hot weather, or during heavy training periods, it should be more. Sports energy drinks are fine, but are usually packed with sugars, so watch out for hidden calories.

On competition days, hydration and gastrointestinal comfort are considerations, so it is important that you feel confident and light. A reduced fibre intake in the final 24 hours is advisable.

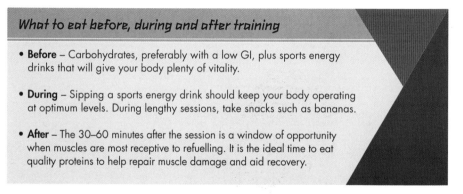

What to eat before, during and after training

- **Before** – Carbohydrates, preferably with a low GI, plus sports energy drinks that will give your body plenty of vitality.

- **During** – Sipping a sports energy drink should keep your body operating at optimum levels. During lengthy sessions, take snacks such as bananas.

- **After** – The 30–60 minutes after the session is a window of opportunity when muscles are most receptive to refuelling. It is the ideal time to eat quality proteins to help repair muscle damage and aid recovery.

The mental edge

Improving your physical condition is not enough. Working on developing a strong mental attitude is essential, especially in jumping and throwing events that can be won or lost during a few seconds of explosive effort.

Sports Psychology

Dedication, determination and the ability to deal with pressure are all traits that can help produce a winning performance. Certainly, the power of the mind can often make the difference between first and second.

The greatest athletes not only have superb natural physical talent, but also display impressive psychological techniques. Much of this comes naturally or was developed during childhood. However, there is also a theory that traits such as self-belief can be trained like anything else.

Sports psychology is definitely not an area to be ignored. It is a travesty, after all, for athletes to work on their strength, speed and technique and then struggle mentally during the competition. Factors such as stress and competitive anxiety have a negative effect on performance, while positive mental traits can turn an average jump or throw into a personal best.

Be Positive

Positive mental traits are often summed up as the 'four Cs': concentration, confidence, control and commitment. There are ways to improve these areas, too. They include:

- **Relaxation** – Stretching and loosening your body, together with deep and slow breathing, will help calm nerves. On the flipside, if you are a relaxed character, you may need to do the opposite to get the adrenalin flowing.
- **Mental imagery** – If you picture success, it will improve your confidence and make you more likely to achieve what you are hoping for.

Three traits shown by world-class athletes

- **Willingness to change** – Top jumpers and throwers are never satisfied with their techniques and will add new ideas and techniques to their programme even if they have recently broken records or won major titles.
- **An obsession with their event** – Modern athletes look to use every moment of the day to improve their performance. Even rest periods are carefully calculated and inserted into their programme.
- **Selfishness** – Leading performers put themselves and their event first. For example, they are far more likely to ignore a night out with friends in favour of an early night.

Before a competition, try to play through the perfect jump or throw in your mind.

- **Goal setting** – Focus your mind by setting short-term and long-term targets.

In addition, confidence can be improved if you carry out your training schedule and remind yourself close to competition of all the hours of work you have done. Spending time with a charismatic coach or enjoying the camaraderie of your training partners can also help.

Finally, remember that athletics is not always about continual improvements. There will be tough times, such as periods of frustration on the sidelines due to injury. How an athlete reacts when that happens is the truest test of all.

An athlete's determination and self-belief can mean the difference between first and second place.

Drugs in sport

With its simple acts of running, jumping and throwing, the sport of athletics has always been susceptible to cheats. One way of gaining an unfair advantage is to take drugs, but it is a route that only the foolhardy take.

Illegal Drug Taking

Cheating occurs in every walk of life and all sports. So athletics is no different and there are always rule-breakers looking to gain an illegal edge.

From the Ancient Greek Olympians who used to bribe competitors, to the endurance athletes at the turn of the last century who took strychnine, through to the state-organised drug programmes of the 1970s and 1980s, cheats have done their best to ruin the history of the sport.

Today, drug cheats are punished with bans, and the shame attached to a positive test is a stigma that an athlete must carry for life.

The most popular types of banned performance-enhancing drugs are:
- **Anabolic steroids and human growth hormone** – to build muscle mass.
- **Stimulants** – to improve alertness and reduce fatigue.
- **Masking drugs** – to prevent the detection of other types of drugs.
- **Painkillers** – to help mask pain.

Drug Testing

Should recreational athletes worry about this? Yes, of course. Drug testing is carried out at every kind of athletics event. This includes national-standard schools meetings through to masters' championships for over-35 athletes. And in recent years a number of veteran athletes at grassroots level have fallen foul of anti-doping rules.

Effects

It is easy to understand why a minority of athletes cheat. Studies have shown that taking steroids can lead to gains of around 2–5 metres in the Shot Put and 10–20m in the Discus. But is it really worth it when the side effects can include cancer, not to mention the shame of being labelled a drug cheat?

Many athletes also believe that taking drugs does not always have the effect the cheats hope for. Indeed, there have been cases where athletes who have cheated have produced better performances during periods when they have been 'clean' than when they were taking drugs.

Medical Conditions

Of course, there are instances where it is OK to take drugs for medical conditions. If this is the case, you need to get a Therapeutic Use Exemption (TUE). One of the most common reasons for obtaining a TUE is if you suffer from asthma.

For more information on performance-enhancing drugs, together with the latest list of banned substances, see the World Anti-Doping Agency website: wada-ama.org

Warning against supplements

Athletes in field events who are searching for speed and strength gains will be tempted to take sports supplements. But be careful. Official advice from sports governing bodies in recent years has warned against using supplements. The reason is that there have been cases where supplements have been contaminated and positive drug tests have resulted.

Athletes should be able to fulfil all of their nutritional requirements from natural food. If you want to risk supplementing your diet with protein powders or energy drinks, though, then buy reputable, well-known brands.

Warming up

A good warm-up will make a great performance and avoidance of injury more likely. So every training session or competition should begin with light aerobic exercise and stretching.

Benefits

Warming up is not a natural instinct. If our prehistoric ancestors were hunting and saw an animal they wanted to kill, then they would run, jump and throw a weapon without a moment's pause. Similarly, children explode into action without any prior preparation.

There are undoubtedly benefits to warming up, however, especially as we get less flexible with age. Stretching itself is very instinctive – humans and many animals often stretch after waking up or long periods of inactivity.

The two main reasons to warm up are:
- To improve performance.
- To reduce the likelihood of injury.

The main goals when warming up are to increase the internal temperature of the body and to increase the flexibility of your joints and muscles. Increasing your range of movement means you will be able to perform better. Imagine, for instance, if your stride was just a few centimetres longer on the runway…

The Warm-up

Warming up should take the first 20–40 minutes of a training session. Start slowly with 5–10 minutes of light exercise such as jogging. This should then be followed by mobility and stretching exercises (see pages 42–3).

Types of stretching

- **Static** – Parts of the body are stretched for a certain amount of time without moving, or by moving very slowly. The muscles are stretched under tension and because of the slow speed this is a safe method for beginners.
- **Passive** – Similar to static stretching but it involves using a partner or apparatus to help further stretch the muscles.
- **Active** – This is performed without the help of any external force. Instead, the stretch happens when the opposing muscles contract and in turn help relax the stretched muscles.
- **Isometric** – Similar to static stretching but contractions are usually held for longer. A classic example is the 'push the wall' calf stretch (see page 43).
- **PNF** – Proprioceptive Neuromuscular Facilitation involves both stretching and contracting the muscle group being targeted.
- **Dynamic and ballistic** – Two techniques that use swinging movements and are definitely not for beginners.

Loosen your joints first before moving on to more specific exercises that stretch muscles and tendons. Particular attention should be given to the parts of the body that will be used most in your chosen event.

When it comes to stretching, this is one of the most debated and controversial issues in athletics. Static stretching is the most common and traditional method used – and should always be done once your body has been warmed up with light exercise. Stretches should be held for 10–20 seconds. Other types of stretching are listed in the panel on page 40.

Finally, the warm-up should conclude with more jogging and then some event-specific work. Jumpers should do strides or bounding. Throwers should carry out some relaxed practice throws.

A thorough warm-up will prevent injury and can improve performance.

Stretching

Stretching is an important part of the warming-up process, and it is important to target all the main body parts when doing your routine.

There are many stretches that can be done when warming up. Ultimately, you will find your favourites and develop a warm-up routine that works for you. But never be afraid to introduce new stretches into your programme. There may also be problem areas in your body, which are perhaps prone to injury, that need extra focus. Here are some popular stretching exercises.

Hamstring (standing)
Put your foot on a knee-high stationary object and slowly lean forward, reaching down the shin until you feel a stretch in the hamstring. Repeat on the other side.

Hamstring (sitting)
Keeping your back flat on the floor and your eyes focused upward, hold the back of your thigh with both hands and (leg bent) pull the thigh into a 90-degree position against the floor and slowly straighten your knee. Repeat on the other side.

Groin
Sit on the floor with the soles of your feet together. Sitting up straight, grasp your feet with your hands. The stretch should be felt in both sides of the groin and down the inside of both thighs.

Hip flexors
Place your feet stride-width apart with the front knee bent. Transfer your body weight forward, pushing your pelvis forward. The stretch should be felt at the front of the hip. Repeat on the other side.

Calf
With both palms flat, lean against a wall. One leg should be back, several feet from the wall, with the heel firmly positioned on the floor. Flex your other leg about halfway between your back leg and the wall. With your back straight, gradually lean forward until you feel the stretch in your calf. Repeat on the other side.

Quadriceps – To balance, hold a stationary object with one hand and use your other hand to grasp your foot or ankle, lifting it toward your bottom. Repeat on the other side.

Triceps – Raise one arm above your head, bent at the elbow and with your hand over your shoulder. Grasp the elbow with your opposite hand and gently push the arm down your back. Repeat on the other side.

Back and shoulders – Place your feet shoulder-width apart and facing forward. With your fingers linked, push your arms straight out with your palms to the front. Twist your arms and push them to one side. The stretch should be felt on the outside of the shoulder and in the centre of the back.

Warming down

Complete a great session by warming down properly. This means more jogging and stretching, and possibly massage and an ice bath, too.

Benefits

Warming down after training or competition is important for many reasons. Like warming up, it is not a natural instinct and the urge might just be to sit down or jump in a car and drive home. But time spent cooling down gradually will have several benefits.

For starters, warming down will help prevent post-exercise soreness. This should be a key goal as you do not want to start the following day – or day's session – being too stiff to move. After working out, there will be an accumulation of waste products like lactic acid in the muscles and this leads to soreness if it is not flushed away. Continuing very light exercise once the main session is over is the best way to speed up the evacuation of this waste.

Secondly, warming down is a great opportunity to improve your flexibility, because after training your muscles and tendons will be fully warmed up. Look on the warming-down process as part of the session itself.

A good warm-down will ensure that lactic acid is flushed from your muscles, your heart rate is back to its resting rate and the level of adrenalin in the blood is back to normal.

The Warm-down

A typical warm-down, therefore, will include some light jogging and then plenty of stretching. The simple rule above all, though, is to keep moving.

If you are still feeling energetic, the warm-down period is also an opportunity to squeeze in some more fitness work. If you have done a big technical session on a runway or in a throwing circle, for instance, then you might begin your warm-down period by doing some sit-ups or press-ups. Or if you have drills you know you need to perform in order to combat an area of your body that is prone to injury, then this is a good time to do them.

Replace fluids as you are warming down by sipping an energy drink. If you are going to be unable to eat for some time, then take a snack – all of which will help the recovery process and allow you to train hard again tomorrow.

Massage might also help the recovery process and is best done when the muscles are already loose and warm.

Finally, when all the stretching is completed, you might be brave enough to step into an ice bath. It will help repair all the micro-damage that the training session has inflicted on your body. Plus, what better way to cool down?

Warming down prevents post-exercise soreness and is a great opportunity to improve your flexibility.

Weights and circuits

Field event athletes spend almost as much time in the gym as in the arena. Here is a beginner's guide to the kind of exercises you can do to build strength.

Building strength and power will help you jump and throw higher and further. These are some popular types of exercise.

Circuit Training

A variety of exercises can be performed over a 30–90-minute period. Athletes, usually in a group, rotate from one station to another with typically 8–15 repetitions at moderate resistance levels (40–60 per cent of maximum).

A sample circuit can include:
- Sprint arms, carrying light dumb-bells (pump your arms vigorously as if sprinting but without moving your legs)
- Plank
- Pull-up
- Forward lunge
- Press-ups
- Step-ups
- Crunches or sit-ups
- Medicine ball bounce on wall
- Burpees

Circuit training, plyometrics and weights all help build the strength and power for both jumping and throwing field events.

Plyometrics

These bounding exercises help to develop elasticity in your muscles and are most used by Jumping athletes. But seek advice from a coach, because inexperienced or young athletes can easily get injured. Examples include:
- **Double-leg bound** – jump over hurdles or cones on a cushioned floor. Jump as far as possible each time and do three to six sets.
- **Lateral hops** – jump left and then right over a bench that is between 30 and 50 centimetres high as many times within a certain time, usually around 20 seconds.
- **Single-leg bound** – similar to the double-leg bound but hopping on one foot.

Weights

Jumpers and throwers wishing to maximise their potential will have to enter into the weights room at some stage. Safety is vital, so make sure you are overseen by a coach. Here are three popular exercises:

- **Bench press** – While lying on a bench with your feet flat on the floor, lift the bar off the rack and lower it to the chest in a steady movement before pressing it back to the starting position. After finishing the desired number of repetitions, return it to the rack. A 'spotter' is useful for safety purposes.

- **Back squat** – Place a bar behind your neck, just above the shoulder blades. With your feet shoulder-width apart and keeping your weight over your ankles, bend your knees and lower your body until your thighs are parallel to the ground. Then straighten your legs back to the original position. Important – keep your back straight throughout.

- **Power clean** – A tough exercise that works most large muscle groups. In the squat position, with your back straight, arms straight and hips at knee height or lower, hold the bar a little wider than shoulder-width, with feet hip-width apart and the bar over your big toes. Drive upward powerfully and keep your back at the same angle until the bar passes your knees. Then, when the bar is at knee height, thrust your hips forward and upward. As the bar passes your hips, rise on the balls of your feet, fully extend your body, shrug your shoulders and bend your elbows upward. From this point, drop quickly into a very slight squat and rotate your hands so that the bar rests on your upturned hands and deltoids.

47

Training troubleshooting

The key potential problems are injury, illness and overtraining. If you are pushing your body to the limit, they are somewhat inevitable, but there are also plenty of solutions.

There will be many difficult issues to overcome as you progress on your athletics journey, but the good news is that you will be able to resolve almost all of them. Here are some common problems and how to solve them.

Illness

Everyone's health takes a knock occasionally, even if it is simply a harmless common cold. Often it is a sign that your body has pushed itself too hard in training. Or perhaps your diet has been poor and left you prone to infection.

What to do?

- Stop training. Or, if you only have a mild head cold, then continue doing light training that does not involve an increase in heart rate or breathing. Eat more fresh fruit to increase the vitamin C in your diet. To help avoid illness close to a competition, regularly wash your hands – especially before eating or after shaking someone's hand.

Overtraining

If you have pushed your body too hard, there will be several warning signs. They include unexpected weight loss, continual tiredness, lack of motivation, inability to concentrate, loss of coordination and lack of appetite.

What to do?

- Quite simply, ease back the training load. Or have a break from specific athletics training by replacing it with a spell of active fitness – in other words, doing some light training in another sport. Consult your coach for the correct training load to ensure you do not overstep the mark again in future.

Injuries

Few athletes go their entire careers without being injured, and jumpers and throwers are particularly prone to physical problems due to the extreme nature of the sport. The Triple Jump, for example, involves a huge amount of pounding, while the Pole Vault carries its own particular risks

What to do?

- If you get injured, stop training straight away. An injury is unlikely to improve if you try to train through it. Seek expert medical help. If the injury is immediate, then ice the affected area.

In order to prevent injuries, make sure you wear decent training, jumping or throwing shoes that have adequate support and cushioning and are not worn out.

When in the gym or weights room, use good footwear and a weights belt to protect your back. Ensure all the equipment is safe. It helps if you have a companion to help 'spot' you in the weights room. And most of all, make certain you are using a sound technique.

In the athletics arena, always be aware of safety issues. Never forget, flying implements can be lethal weapons.

Finally, warm up properly and stretch thoroughly. A weak body is also more likely to suffer injury, so spend enough time doing general strength and conditioning work before you take to the runway or circle.

Injuries will be an unfortunate part of your athletics journey, but with care they can be kept to a minimum.

Field disciplines in detail

Excelling in your chosen field event requires specific training. So here we take a step-by-step look at each discipline, with advice on technique and training.

High Jump

Leading high jumpers often have a unique type of build in order to help them spring and curve over the bar. Proper footwear is also essential in this event.

Olympic History

The art of jumping over a horizontal bar placed at measured heights dates back to the Ancient Greek Olympic Games. Over the years, though, techniques have become more effective, leading to top athletes being able to clear a mark that is taller than their own height.

The High Jump relies less on speed than the other Jumping events and those who use the popular 'Flop' technique also follow a curved path before taking off over the bar.

Ideal Physical Qualities

High jumpers often have tall and slim bodies – an ideal shape for rising and gliding over the bar. While it certainly helps, huge height is not an absolute necessity, though. Stefan Holm of Sweden, the 2004 Olympic champion, has jumped more than half a metre over his own height of 5 feet 11½ inches (1.81m), and heptathlete Jessica Ennis is one of the United Kingdom's best high jumpers despite standing only 5ft 5in tall (1.65m).

Whatever body type, successful high jumpers must have great spring in their legs and the ability to perform a back arch over the bar. This kind of flexibility is developed in training.

Clothing and Footwear

Due to the modern curved approach

Blanka Vlašic

At 6ft 4in (1.93m) tall, the slender Croatian is ideally built for the High Jump event. Good genes also help, as her father was an international decathlete and her mother a basketball player.

During her youth she wanted to be a sprinter, but instead she showed more talent in the High Jump and won the world junior title in 2000 and 2002 in addition to competing in the Sydney 2000 Olympic Games aged 16.

Since then, Blanka – who is named after the city Casablanca – has won World and European titles.

before take-off with the Fosbury Flop technique, the type of footwear worn is vital. Specialist High Jump shoes have spikes not only on the sole but also on the heel in order to prevent slipping during the final stride before jumping. Related to this, many athletes wear short spikes – or even none at all – on the leading leg that swings up.

Clothing is simple – a traditional athletics singlet and shorts are standard fare. Remember to keep warm pre-training and competition, too, with a good tracksuit and wet-weather gear.

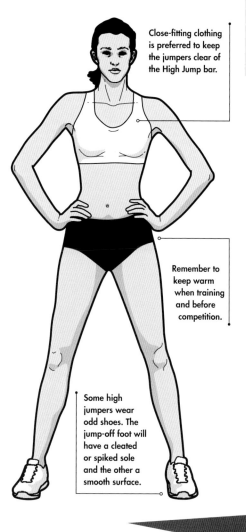

Close-fitting clothing is preferred to keep the jumpers clear of the High Jump bar.

Remember to keep warm when training and before competition.

Some high jumpers wear odd shoes. The jump-off foot will have a cleated or spiked sole and the other a smooth surface.

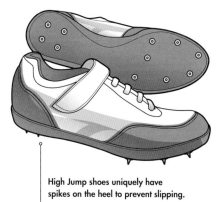

High Jump shoes uniquely have spikes on the heel to prevent slipping.

Indoor Jumping

High Jump is also a popular event during the indoor season, which takes place mainly from January to March. So many high jumpers tweak their technique with some low-key competitions during the winter months.

Jumping in the rain is usually a miserable affair anyway, so athletes always relish the chance to perform in dry and warm conditions.

Standards to Aspire to

	Senior	U20	U17	U15	U13
Men	1.73m	1.70m	1.65m	1.50m	1.25m
Women	1.50m	1.50m	1.45m	1.36m	1.20m

High Jump in the arena

Deciding the result of a High Jump competition is simple – it is the athlete who jumps highest. But there are several other rules and safety tips to consider before you start.

Arena Facts

The High Jump takes place at one end of the arena, with the athletes jumping over a fibreglass bar that is about 4 metres long and supported by rigid uprights. Minimum lengths of the runway range from 15m to 25m, while the landing mat is at least 5m long and 3m wide.

Jumping

Athletes fail an attempt if the bar falls off as a result of their attempt. Jumps are also ruled out if athletes put their arms under the bar during the jump or touch the landing mat before they have gone over the bar.

Athletes are allowed to abort an attempt before take-off and then repeat, just as long as the whole process happens within a set time limit, but retaking an attempt is not allowed if athletes break the vertical plane between the uprights.

During competition, athletes jump until they have failed three successive times – and these can be at various heights. Athletes can begin at any height at, or above, the original starting height and can miss certain heights if they wish.

In the event of a tie, the athlete with the fewest failures at the best height cleared is given the top position. If the athletes are still tied, the athlete with the fewest failures is given the leading spot.

On the scorecards, clearances are marked with a letter 'o'. Failures are shown with an 'x'. So athletes might be given the following scores next to their names:

Name/height	2.05m	2.09m	2.12m	2.15m
Wenlock	o	o	xo	xxx
Mandeville	o	xo	xxo	xxx

Athletes continue in the High Jump until they fail three successive times.

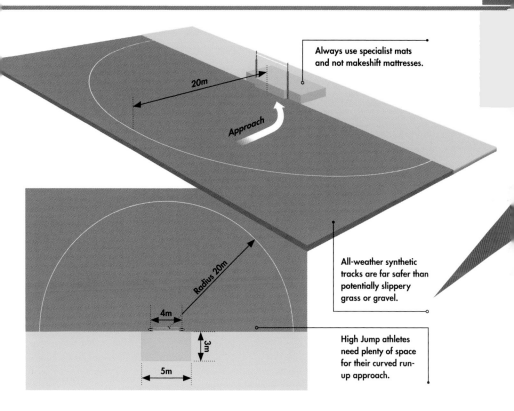

Always use specialist mats and not makeshift mattresses.

20m

Approach

Radius 20m

4m

3m

5m

All-weather synthetic tracks are far safer than potentially slippery grass or gravel.

High Jump athletes need plenty of space for their curved run-up approach.

Safety

Most athletes use the Fosbury Flop technique, so they land on their shoulders and the backs of their necks. Given this, the landing mat must not be too low to the ground in relation to the height being jumped, otherwise too much over-rotation will take place, potentially leading to injury – specialist High Jump landing mats must be used that are at least 1m or more above ground level. Never create makeshift landing mats out of gymnastic pads or similar items.

During training, rubber tubes are often preferred to fibreglass competition bars.

If these are used, you should ensure that the standards do not get dragged inward if the tubing is hit.

Finally, High Jump practice is safest when carried out on an all-weather track. Grass or artificial surfaces are potentially slippery. Specialist High Jump spikes are recommended, too.

Key Rules
- The bar is raised by 5cm, 3cm or 2cm increments.
- Double-footed take-offs are not allowed.

High Jump techniques explained

During the evolution of the High Jump, the technique used to clear the bar has undergone many changes. In fact, when it comes to the methods used by athletes, the High Jump probably has the most colourful history of any event in the sport.

The Fosbury Flop, invented by 1968 Olympic champion Dick Fosbury, is the technique that has come to be used by the vast majority of today's athletes. It is the method that has proved to bring the best height possible. For young athletes it is a dramatic and attractive option, too.

How to 'Flop'

Approach runs in the Flop are longer and quicker than for other styles – usually 8–12 strides – and the run-up is curved during the final few strides (see page 58). This curving action leads to rotation about the vertical axis as athletes leave the ground, helping them to pass over the bar and land on their backs. The Flop is therefore able to utilise good horizontal speed, but the athlete then needs to turn in the air and, above all, a good take-off position is vital.

The Fosbury Flop

The athlete takes off with the foot furthest from the bar and the free leg is a bent one. When airborne, the body should be turned into a loose backward arch, with the head and heels pulled in. The legs and feet are then brought over the bar with carefully timed straightening of the limbs. The athlete then lands on the upper back and shoulders.

Straddle Jump

This was the dominant style before the Flop became popular and some athletes still use it. Using a straight approach run, the athlete takes off with the foot that is closest to the bar. Once airborne, the athlete then rotates, stomach

Maintain a tall posture and do not slow down approaching the bar.

Aim for a consistent tempo and stride pattern during the run-up.

Raise your arms vertically and into the bar.

The Scissors Jump

face down, to finally land on their back.

An athlete using this technique held the world record as recently as 1978.

Scissors Jump

Jumping into a sandpit or on to a landing mat that is not the correct height is not recommended. But during the early days of the High Jump there were no soft landing mats, which meant this technique was very popular as it allowed athletes to land on their feet.

The athlete runs briskly towards the bar at a slight angle with the shoulders held high and then, at take-off (pushing off with the foot furthest away from the

Scissors Jump – push off with the leg furthest from the jump, whilst swinging the other leg straight so it clears the bar.

bar), the drive leg (nearest the bar) is held straight and swung into the air to clear the bar. Meanwhile, the take-off leg drives the body into the air and as the jumper crosses the bar the take-off leg has to be swung fast to clear the bar.

The term scissors arises from the fact that the drive leg pushes downward after it has cleared the bar, while the take-off leg swings upward.

Other Techniques

These methods have been used at various stages throughout history as the event has modernised:

- **Eastern Cut-off** – Very similar to the scissors approach, but athletes lean backward as they go over the bar, landing on their shoulders on a mat.
- **Western Roll** – The run-up is at a slight angle to the bar and the inner leg is used for the take-off, while the outer leg is thrust up to lead the body sideways over the bar.

Arch your back and push hips upward when going over the bar.

Bring legs and feet over the bar with perfect timing.

Relax your body as you land on your back and shoulders.

High Jump training tips and techniques

Assuming most budding high jumpers are going to pursue the perfection of the Flop method, here are some more detailed technical tips for you to try in your training.

As you carry out the Fosbury Flop (see page 56), there are several important things to work on during training. Firstly, it is vital to focus on the approach run above all else. By the time you leave the ground, there is little that can be done to change the end result. Therefore, achieving a solid run-up will help enormously.

Approach Run

Practise your run-up repeatedly, concentrating on a consistent tempo and stride pattern. The best speed differs from one athlete to another. Too fast and the leg will buckle and vertical transition will be difficult; too slow and the stretch reflexes will not be stimulated enough and there will not be enough energy to complete the rotations over the bar. Above all, you must never slow down before taking off.

The run-up should be curved – in the shape of a letter 'J' – and with a lateral lean away from the bar at take-off. The straight part of the run-up during the first five or seven strides ensures speed is achieved. Once the curved part of the 'J' approach begins, keep a tall posture and fast leg turnover.

Take-off

Strive to achieve a low hip position during the final strides of the run-up without slowing down. In the crucial penultimate step, your ankle and knee should be flexed, with the foot remaining under the hips, and your body should lean away from the bar.

Jumpers mark their run-up so that every approach is consistent.

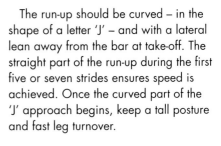

A consistent approach run and precision take-off are the fundamentals of High Jump success.

When the shoulders cross the bar, your back should be arched and your hips pushed upward. When your bottom passes over the bar, flex your hips and bring your legs up toward the chest. As you land on your back and shoulders, relax your body.

As you become more experienced, a double-arm action can be blended into the technique in order to propel the body upward on take-off. Your arms should be raised vertically and not into the bar.

Finally, avoid the temptation to look directly at the bar.

Training Tips

- The majority of training should focus on the run-up.
- It is advisable to start from a standing position and it is useful to use a checkmark such as tape. Every effort should be made to make every run-up exactly the same, regardless of the height of the bar.
- Count your strides as you approach the bar.
- Technique aside, work on flexibility and leg power in training.

Pole Vault

Pole vaulters need speed, strength and gymnastic ability to allow them to sail over ever-greater heights using a high-tech pole, which has changed hugely since the event took place at the first modern Olympic Games in Athens in 1896.

Olympic History

The origins of the Pole Vault lie with men who used sticks to clear obstacles such as ditches or streams. Today, confident and competent athletes use modern equipment to clear heights that are as high as a house. Despite being in the first modern Olympic Games, though, the first women's Pole Vault was not included until Sydney 2000.

Ideal Physical Qualities

Top pole vaulters have speed, great upper-body strength, poise, flexibility and fearlessness. Not surprisingly, many pole vaulters have a background in gymnastics.

Clothing and Footwear

When it comes to gear, specialist shoes are available but traditional sprint spikes can also be worn, plus a standard singlet and vest. Many pole vaulters, however, use a resin or chalk on their hands for a better

Pole vaulters use resin or chalk on their hands to improve their grip.

Yelena Isinbayeva

The Russian won the women's Olympic title at both the Athens 2004 and Beijing 2008 Games, and holds the world record. Consequently, she is widely regarded as being the greatest pole vaulter in the short history of the women's event.

Like many successful pole vaulters, she has a background in gymnastics and this has helped her develop a technique that top coaches have described as being on a par with the best men in the world.

grip. For safety, some athletes also wear small helmets.

Safety

Safety in the Pole Vault is very important. Like in the High Jump, vaulters should land in a relaxed fashion on their shoulders and backs – and on specialist Pole Vault mats, too, because High Jump mats are not cushioned enough.

Rubber tubing is also recommended during practice sessions instead of a firm crossbar, as is using the correct type of pole for your height and weight.

Slippery weather causes problems, although the Pole Vault benefits from being part of the indoor circuit. Indoors or out, some athletes even wear small head guards.

Good coaching, naturally, is also vital in order to avoid accidents. But on the plus side, remember that pole vaulters of yesteryear used to land in sand, grass or sawdust!

Standards to Aspire to

	Senior	U20	U17	U15	U13
Men	3.00m	2.80m	2.65m	2.20m	2.00m
Women	2.40m	2.30m	2.20m	2.00m	1.90m

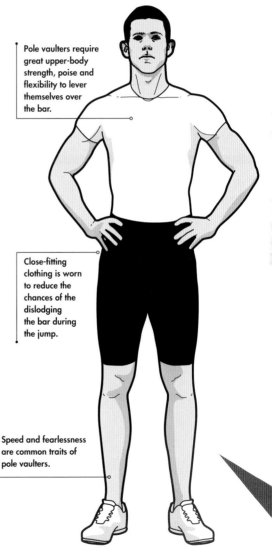

Pole vaulters require great upper-body strength, poise and flexibility to lever themselves over the bar.

Close-fitting clothing is worn to reduce the chances of the dislodging the bar during the jump.

Speed and fearlessness are common traits of pole vaulters.

Pole vaulters wear spiked running shoes for extra grip on their run-up.

Pole Vault in the arena

The Pole Vault is arguably the most spectacular event in the athletics arena. Athletes use a mix of athleticism and bravery as they launch themselves over a high bar using a pole.

The Pole

Modern poles are graded according to the amount of weight that will cause them to bend at a certain height. Poles are made out of fibreglass or carbon fibre and can be any size or weight – and range from between 3 and 5 metres in length – and they can also vary in stiffness.

The binding tape that athletes grip is not allowed to be more than two layers thick.

Arena Facts

Athletes begin their attempt down a runway that is at least 40m long and around 1.25m wide. They then place the end of the pole into a box that is sunk level with the runway and 1m in length, measured along the inside of the bottom of the box, 60 centimetres in width at the front end and tapering to 15cm in width at the bottom of the back board.

The crossbar, which is made of fibreglass and is 4.5m long, rests on two pegs. The landing area is not less than 6m long and 6m wide, plus 80cm high.

Jumping

At the start of the competition, athletes must declare their opening height. Athletes fail an attempt if the bar falls off as a result of their vault. It will also be a disallowed vault if the athlete touches the ground, including the landing area, beyond the vertical plane through the back end of the box, with any part of the body or pole, without first clearing the bar.

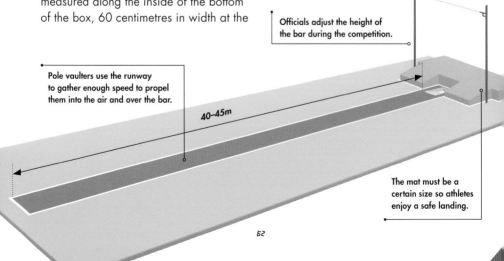

Officials adjust the height of the bar during the competition.

Pole vaulters use the runway to gather enough speed to propel them into the air and over the bar.

40–45m

The mat must be a certain size so athletes enjoy a safe landing.

Athletes are, however, allowed to run outside the white lines marking the runway and the pole can also touch the landing mat after it has been properly planted in the box. Similarly, if a pole suffers a rare break during an attempt, the athlete will be given a new attempt.

Like High Jump, competitors continue to vault until they have failed three successive times – and these can be at various heights. Athletes can also begin at any height at, or above, the original starting height and can miss certain heights if they wish.

In the event of a tie, the athlete with the fewest failures at the best height cleared is given the top position. If athletes are still tied, the athlete with the fewest failures is given the leading spot.

On the scorecards, clearances are marked with a letter 'o'. Failures are shown with an 'x'. In the case of total failure, the initials 'NH' – for 'no height' – are used.

Key Rules

- Vaulters are allowed two minutes to complete an attempt.
- During the vault the athlete is not allowed to go above the grip taken by the upper hand after take-off.
- The bar is never raised by less than 5cm after each round of trials.
- Replacing the bar with hands while airborne – a tricky technique known as 'volzing' – is banned.

Vaulters plant their pole into a sunken box.

Modern poles are made out of fibreglass or carbon fibre and have led to big improvements in heights cleared.

Pole Vault techniques explained

The Pole Vault is a complex technical event and here we look at the approach run, plant into the box and initial take-off. Under the supervision of a coach, follow these steps to get the most out of your potential.

There are several phases in the Pole Vault – the approach run, the plant, the take-off, the swing-up (or ride) and, finally, the bar clearance. Athletes use slight variations of technique, but the basic and most popular methods are explained below.

Approach Run

Right handed vaulters grip the pole with their right hand nearer the top, carry it on their right-hand side and take off from the left foot. Left-handed vaulters do the opposite.

For a right-handed vaulter, the left hand is positioned just above waist height and about 2.5 centimetres in front of the hips. The right hand is positioned at the rear of the hips with the palm facing forward and it also presses down to balance the weight of the pole and ensure the front end rises off the ground. Both hands are shoulder-width apart. The angle that the pole is held at is one of personal preference.

The athlete then runs in a relaxed fashion, gradually lowering the pole and aiming to hit top speed just before planting the pole in the box. This usually comes after about 20 strides.

Keep your right arm straight and left arm slightly bent during take-off.

Hold the pole with your right hand nearer the top if you are right-handed.

Plant

This action starts on the third to last stride, with the athlete pushing the pole forward with the aim of transferring energy accumulated during the run-up into potential energy stored by the elasticity of the pole.

The arms are raised from hip height until they are outstretched above the head. At this moment, the tip of the pole drops into the box.

Take-off

With the right arm straight and left arm slightly flexed (for a right-handed vaulter), the lead leg drives upward and the trail leg is straightened and stays in an extended position.

At this point the pole will bend, an action that will result in the athlete being propelled over the bar. After a moment where the athlete extends and hangs on to the pole, they then flex their waist and start to pull upward.

Technique Tips

- Ensure the grip is firm, with hands shoulder-width apart.
- Accelerate during the run-up, and run tall with high knees.
- Push the pole forward and upward, taking off with the body directly below an extended right arm.
- Keep the take-off foot under the top hand when leaving the ground.
- Flex the pole with the forward push of the lower arm together with the downward push of the upper arm.

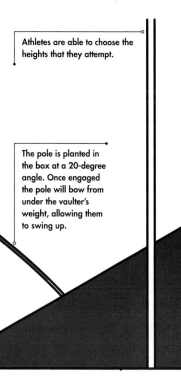

Athletes are able to choose the heights that they attempt.

The pole is planted in the box at a 20-degree angle. Once engaged the pole will bow from under the vaulter's weight, allowing them to swing up.

For safety purposes, never use makeshift or home-made landing mats. Foam rubber is usually used and the mat has a minimum thickness of 1–1.5 metres.

Pole Vault techniques explained

The final stages of the Pole Vault involve the swing-up and clearance over the bar followed, of course, by a safe landing. Then, if everything has gone right, the bar will still be in place.

Swing-Up

The athlete's chest leads, with the left leg held back; the bent pole delivers the energy needed to get up and over the bar. The left arm is not rigid but turns outward slightly and the right arm is straight and is left behind. Then, as the pole begins to straighten, the athlete goes upside down as the feet are driven upward, close to the pole and towards the bar.

This is achieved by the arms pulling the pole to the chest, allied to the legs being pushed upward. The stage is often called the 'rock back'.

The centre of gravity remains as low as possible until the bend of the pole is at its greatest in order to gain maximum horizontal distance. When the pole is at its maximum bending point, this is where the hips begin to swing up.

The hips move forward as the bent leg straightens and joins the straight leg. The athlete is now in a pike position, with feet together and both arms remaining straight.

During this phase there are different ways to achieve the swing-up. A 'double-leg drop' technique is popular, as is a method called the 'tuck and shoot'.

Clearance

A slight rotation will ensure the athlete adopts a face-down position above the bar. As the pole straightens, helping the athlete's height in the air, the back arches as the athlete pushes away from the pole, over the bar and into a relaxed fall on to the mats.

The athlete lets go of the pole with the left hand and extends the right arm so that it virtually becomes an extension of the pole. Officials, meanwhile, are able to catch the pole as it falls down.

The pole is pulled to the chest as the legs swing up as the bent pole delivers energy required to get over the bar.

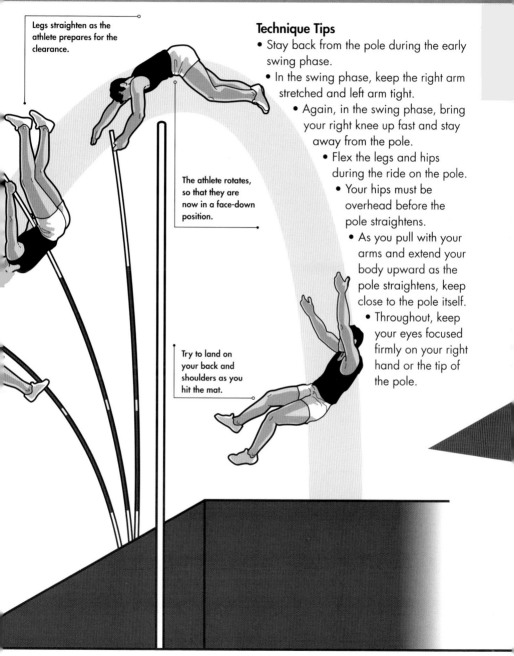

Legs straighten as the athlete prepares for the clearance.

The athlete rotates, so that they are now in a face-down position.

Try to land on your back and shoulders as you hit the mat.

Technique Tips
- Stay back from the pole during the early swing phase.
- In the swing phase, keep the right arm stretched and left arm tight.
- Again, in the swing phase, bring your right knee up fast and stay away from the pole.
- Flex the legs and hips during the ride on the pole.
- Your hips must be overhead before the pole straightens.
- As you pull with your arms and extend your body upward as the pole straightens, keep close to the pole itself.
- Throughout, keep your eyes focused firmly on your right hand or the tip of the pole.

Pole Vault training tips and techniques

Pole Vault is definitely not an event that amateurs should dabble with unsupervised. Join a club, find a good coach and build up your strength and confidence gradually.

Pole vaulters such as Yelena Isinbayeva and the great Sergey Bubka are not only hugely admired in their own event but also widely regarded as being among the greatest athletes ever – throughout the whole track and field programme. The absolute pinnacle of world-class vaulting for men is to surpass 6 metres. So start training now and, if you have the talent and desire, it might be possible to achieve this in several years' time.

To achieve anywhere near this level of ability, in addition to huge natural talent you will need to undertake many hours of sprint work, jumping or plyometrics, and gymnastics. Indeed, many pole vaulters spend lots of time working on traditional gymnastics skills – using parallel bars, rings and ropes to build strength and coordination.

Rope Drill

This is a common exercise that develops your upper body strength and mimics the way you pull on the pole during the vault itself. A simple climb up a knotted rope is good for starters – although it is better to do lots of short climbs as opposed to long, high ones.

Next, swing on a rope and lift the knees up – similar to the action during the swing-up stage of the Pole Vault. Try and touch the rope with your knees and feet. Again, do not go too high, and place mats below as a safety precaution.

This is just one of many drills that can be performed and a good Pole Vault coach will be able to oversee others.

Common Faults and Remedies

- If there is inconsistency in the run-up, then remeasure the distance and see if the speed running back from the take-off point is the same as the speed used in the approach run. Run-ups that are inconsistent can be helped by practising with a shorter run-up and improving sprinting ability.
- Poles that do not flex when you vault are generally not the correct type for your size and strength.
- If the legs are not elevated during the swing-up phase, the upper arm should be extended and the legs raised by dropping the shoulders back. Extra strength work on the abdominals and upper body might be necessary.
- If you and the pole fail to rise to a vertical position, this is possibly due to not sprinting quickly enough during the approach.
- Young athletes have different levels of ability and confidence. So coaches should approach group training sessions with care.

If the pole does not flex, perhaps you need to get a different type that matches your size and strength.

Long Jump

Great long jumpers have superb sprinting speed and leg strength to leap from the board. But good technique and timing are also vital.

Olympic History

Long Jump is an attractive option for budding athletes, partly due to its rich history. It was, after all, one of the five events in the original Pentathlon in the Ancient Greek Olympic Games. Back then, athletes often carried small hand weights – called 'halteres' – which helped them jump further as they threw their fists down and backward during the jump. Music was often played during competitions as the athletes attempted to find a rhythm and master the technique of swinging the weights in order to shift their centre of gravity during the jump.

Over the years athletes have been restricted to shorter run-ups – and, in the case of the early Modern Olympic Games, the Standing Long Jump was an official event until Stockholm 1912.

The Long Jump for women was not added to the Olympic programme until Amsterdam 1928. Since then the event has progressed rapidly, with leading women jumping over 7 metres compared to the 8m-plus elite men.

Ideal Physical Qualities

Throughout the history of Athletics, the Long Jump has often been dominated by athletes who have also been world-class sprinters. Jesse Owens famously won 100m, 200m, 4x100m and Long Jump gold medals at

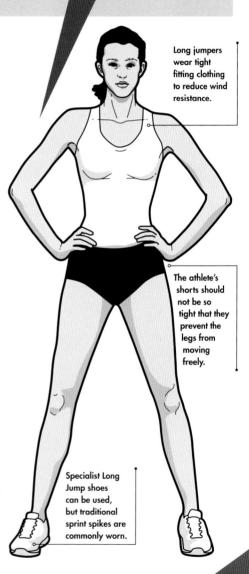

Long jumpers wear tight fitting clothing to reduce wind resistance.

The athlete's shorts should not be so tight that they prevent the legs from moving freely.

Specialist Long Jump shoes can be used, but traditional sprint spikes are commonly worn.

the Berlin Olympic Games in 1936.

But the event has also featured many great athletes who were not renowned for achievements in sprinting. Bob Beamon, for example, was a specialist long jumper and won Olympic gold at the Mexico 1968 Games with a huge 8.9m.

Many current athletes are specialist long jumpers, too. Leading British long jumpers such as Chris Tomlinson and Jade Johnson, for instance, are good sprinters who are more at home charging down a runway.

Clothing and Footwear

As for kit and gear, specialist Long Jump shoes can be worn, but traditional sprint spikes are acceptable. A standard athletics singlet and shorts are also the usual attire.

Spiked shoes give Long Jump competitors the grip to achieve fast run-ups.

Standards to Aspire to

	Senior	U20	U17	U15	U13
Men	5.80m	5.70m	5.40m	4.80m	4.00m
Women	4.75m	4.65m	4.60m	4.30m	3.80m

Mike Powell

During a titanic clash with fellow American Carl Lewis at the 1991 International Association of Athletics Federations World Championships in Tokyo, Mike Powell smashed Bob Beamon's long-standing world Long Jump record with a leap of 8.95m.

The clash with Lewis in Tokyo is widely regarded as one of the most dramatic field event competitions ever. Later, Powell returned to win the world title in Stuttgart in 1993 but he was the 'nearly man' at Olympic level, winning silver at both the Seoul 1988 and Barcelona 1992 Olympic Games behind Lewis.

Long Jump in the arena

At first glance, the Long Jump looks simple. But there is more to it than meets the eye and one challenge is to pick the right technique before you start competing.

Arena Facts

The runway is usually parallel to one of the straights of the running track. The take-off board is usually white and made of wood so that the athlete's spikes will not slip on it, and it is 1–3 metres from the start of the landing area and at least 10m from the end of the area.

Plasticine is often used in front of the take off board to help officials tell whether a jump was a foul. If a mark is made, in the Plasticine after an attempt is made then this is rolled over, or, to avoid delays, a spare strip of Plasticine is often used. If no Plasticine is available, an official will use eyesight to determine whether the jump was legal or not.

The landing area is between 2.75m and 3m wide, and is filled with soft and preferably damp sand, with the top of it level with the take-off board. After each jump, the sand is smoothed over with a rake by officials.

Key Rules

The distance measured is from the take-off board to the part of the mark in the sand that is nearest the board. If an athlete jumps from beyond the take-off board, it is a foul.

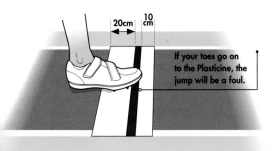

20cm · 10 cm

If your toes go on to the Plasticine, the jump will be a foul.

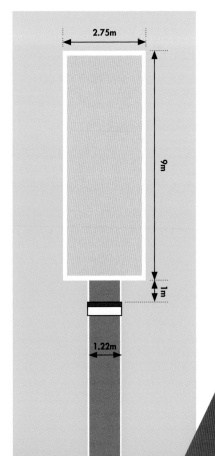

2.75m

9m

1m

1.22m

40–45m

The runway must be long enough for athletes to reach top speed.

Jumping

The Long Jump is one of two horizontal jumps in Athletics – the other being the Triple Jump – and sees competitors sprinting down a runway before jumping as far as they can from a take-off board into a sandpit.

Athletes are not allowed to place markers on the runway to remind them where their run-up begins, but they are able to place markers – or pieces of tape – right at the side of the runway.

Athletes can jump from as far behind the take-off board – or foul line – as they wish, but the distance measured is from the board to the nearest mark made in the sand that is closest to the board.

If the athlete jumps from beyond the take-off board, the jump is judged to be a foul (see opposite).

Athletes usually have three jumps and their best effort is the one that counts. In some competitions the best athletes go forward into what is effectively a second round of jumps, with a further three jumps. If this happens, the best mark in all six rounds wins.

Wind speeds are often taken and if the speed during a jump is measured at greater than 2m per second the jump will be allowed to stand in the competition but will not be accepted for record purposes.

On landing, athletes must not exit back through the sandpit. If they do, and leave a mark closer to the take-off board than their jump, that will be the one used for measuring.

Long Jump techniques explained

Long Jump technique is often neglected by athletes and coaches who mistakenly believe that little more than fast running is necessary. Long Jump technique can be split into four parts: the approach run, the take-off, the flight and the landing.

Approach Run

Speed built during this phase is what gives the Jump good distance. And, in turn, the approach can be split into three distinct parts:

1. The beginning of the run-up is characterised by rapid acceleration and a forward lean of the athlete.
2. During this mid-phase, speed reaches a high level and the athlete begins to run more upright.
3. At the conclusion of the run-up the leg speed reaches its peak and the athlete maintains good form.

An athlete usually needs 18–22 strides during the run-up. Faster runners might need more than this in order to have enough time to hit top speed.

Younger athletes, however, will often reach top speed early during the approach – and therefore often need a shorter run-up – whereas older athletes take longer to reach full pace.

The start of the approach run should be marked and made from a standing start to ensure consistency.

Take-off

A high hip position is crucial and strong vertical actions by the free leg and opposing arm. The hips sink slightly during the penultimate strides and are then raised at the last moment. The penultimate strides will also be

Athletes take 18–22 strides before take off.

Take off at an angle of about 20–25 degrees.

Limbs can be used during flight to increase distance.

longer than usual, but the final stride slightly shorter.

When the take-off foot is placed on the board, it is slightly in advance of the hips and should strike the board on the midline.

The foot plant should also be relatively flat and not on the heel. As for take-off angle, the best one is not 45 degrees, as you might think, but rather around 20–25 degrees.

Flight

Good horizontal speed together with a powerful leap results in a good distance. But the flight stage is when legs and arms can be used to prevent athletes landing early. Different techniques can be used, which are explained on pages 76–7.

Landing

The basic goal is to keep the heels as far away from the take-off board as possible. As the feet hit the sand, the heels are pressed downward and the hamstrings contracted, causing the hips to rise. Then the hips twist to one side and the forward momentum carries the body past the landing position.

The body should not fall back behind the point where the heels hit the sand.

Technique Tips

- Aim for maximum speed in the run-up.
- Lower your hips in the penultimate stride and then raise them to maximum height at take-off.
- Keep the foot flat when jumping. Hitting with your heel first will cause a braking action, while jumping on the toes will lead to energy being lost as the ankle flexes.
- Prevent forward rotation when airborne. Put your feet horizontally at full distance away from your hips when landing.

Various techniques can be used while in the air.

Prepare to hit the sand and do not fall back.

Heels are pressed into the sand and hips twist to one side.

Long Jump flight techniques explained

Not much can be done to change where athletes will land once they have taken off. But there are four types of technique that can influence how long jumpers land in the pit – the sail, the the hang, hitch-kick and the stride jump.

The Sail

This is a very simple style favoured by beginners. The knees are tucked up to the chest, with athletes almost reaching out to touch their toes.

It is not considered the most effective technique, however. This is because if the legs are fully extended and held as long as possible, the body can rotate too far forward. This early rotation can actually cause the legs to drop prematurely, losing valuable distance.

The Hang

Both legs trail the body while it is airborne before being brought forward at the final moment before landing. As the body is lengthened out as much as possible, the athlete 'hangs' in the air for a moment, hence the name.

On take-off the arms go overhead to slow down any rotation that might occur around the athlete's centre of gravity. The legs then lift upward and forward and the arms swing past the legs as the athlete lands to make sure there is a good leg shoot.

The Hitch-kick

The legs continue in a running action during flight, with one rotation for inexperienced or weaker jumpers and two rotations for stronger and more experienced athletes.

After the take-off, the free leg is swung back straight. Meanwhile, the take-off leg folds under the hips and moves forward, at first bending and then straightening before landing. Having completed its backward swing, the free leg then folds and moves forward, bending at the knee, ready to join the take-off leg as the athlete lands in the sand.

This is a difficult style for beginners as they will be unable to reach the distance required to complete the movements.

Stride Jump

The leading leg and take-off leg are kept separate for as long as possible. This gives a stable flight position prior to landing.

In short, the take-off position is held for as long as possible, with the leg that pushed off the board being brought to join the free leg at the final moment.

This is perhaps the best technique for beginners, as it is simple to learn and can be modified into the more advanced hitch-kick at a later stage.

The Sail

The Hang

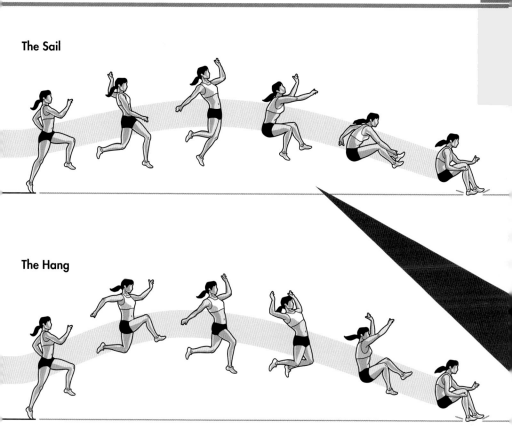

The Hitch-kick

Long Jump training tips and techniques

Long jumpers should spend time perfecting their chosen technique. Yet general sprint, strength and conditioning training are also important if you are going to maximise your potential.

In the same way that a Marathon runner does not run 26 miles at race pace every day in training, field event athletes do not simply practise competition-style efforts over and over again. Instead, they do lots of supplementary training.

This is especially true in the Long Jump, as even top athletes might only practise the full technique two or three times per week. The rest of the time is spent sprint training, bounding, doing drills, lifting weights and doing flexibility exercises.

Bounding exercises are particularly useful and specific to improving Long Jump performance. There are simple exercises such as single leg bounds or double leg bounds (see page 46). Here are some other useful exercises:

Jumping into sand only forms a small part of a long jumper's training.

If athletes are struggling to hit the take-off board, then mark out a much larger zone from which to leap from in order to improve confidence.

Jumping from Beat Board and Low Box

With a three-stride run-up, bounce from a gymnastic-style beat board and on to a low box, then take off from your favourite leg before landing on a soft mat or sand. Drive up strongly from the box and swing the arms upward and forward as vigorously as you can.

Standing Jump over Sand

Make a mound of sand lengthways down the sandpit, then try to jump across it with a double-foot hop from a standing start. Extend the legs at take-off before flexing them fast to get over the top of the mound. Then extend them forward for landing.

Use a Take-off Zone

If you get demoralised by failing to precisely hit the Long Jump take-off board, then mark out a larger zone. If you jump from anywhere within this zone, it will reduce the pressure of hitting an exact mark and increase the fun factor.

Common faults

- If you stutter and take off on the wrong foot, remeasure the run-up and checkmarks, and aim for a consistent run-up every time.
- If you jump well vertically but not very far horizontally you should practise jumping with the penultimate stride on a beat board before leaping off a low vaulting box.
- If you fail to achieve much height, practise bounding exercises and try to improve your leg strength in the gym and weights room.
- If you fall back into the sand on landing, remember to flex the knees when your feet hit the sand and throw the arms forward.

Triple Jump

One of the toughest events on the Athletics programme, the Triple Jump should be approached with caution by young or inexperienced athletes. Once mastered, though, it is dramatic to watch and exciting to take part in.

Olympic History

The origins of the Triple Jump can be traced back to the Ancient Greek Olympic Games, and it was also an event in the first Modern Athens 1896 Games, albeit with a slightly different format of 'hop, hop, jump' instead of the current 'hop, step, jump'.

Like Long Jump, there were also competitions from a standing position. But Triple Jump has only recently become a popular event for women and did not make its Olympic debut until the Atlanta 1996 Games – a full century after men won Olympic medals at the inaugural Modern Games.

Ideal Physical Qualities

Triple jumpers are among the most dynamic athletes in the sport.

They must have the pace of a sprinter to be able to generate enough speed down the runway. Their legs must be strong enough to propel them to distances as great as 15–18 metres. In addition, superb balance and rhythm are needed in order to time the jump to perfection.

To do this, triple jumpers must be able to balance their effort throughout the entire jump. They must also possess the ability to jump and 'rebound' three times in succession.

Standards to Aspire to

	Senior	U20	U17	U15	U13
Men	11.80m	11.50m	11.00m	10.00m	9.00m
Women	9.50m	9.25m	9.00m	8.50m	–

Jonathan Edwards

Jonathan Edwards did everything as a triple jumper. He won the European, Commonwealth, World and Olympic titles – the latter coming at the Sydney Games in 2000.

More than that, though, he is remembered for his tremendous world record of 18.29m, which was set at the 1995 IAAF World Championships in Gothenburg. The Gateshead Harriers athlete also jumped a mammoth 18.43m in Lille in 1995, but the wind speed was over the allowable limit.

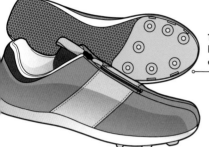

Triple Jump shoes have spikes for extra grip.

Triple jumpers wear tight fitting clothing to reduce wind resistance.

Clothing and Footwear

When it comes to footwear, special Triple Jump spikes offer cushioning and support to withstand the extreme pounding that the athlete's limbs will have to endure. Due to the tough nature of the event, many injuries can easily occur and extreme stress can be put on the knees, ankles, heels and hips. So good footwear is essential to help avoid injury, while proper strength and conditioning can also combat the niggles that might occur.

Not only do specialist shoes protect the legs from heavy impact, they are also designed to prevent sand getting into the shoe!

As with the Long Jump, it is important that the athlete's legs can move freely and their clothing isn't restrictive.

Indoor Jumping

As with all jumps, the Triple Jump is part of the indoor circuit, too, and many athletes spend their off-season period fine-tuning their technique at special indoor arenas where the temperatures are constant and there is no wind or inclement weather to affect the athlete's run-up.

Triple Jump shoes are specially cushioned to reduce the impact of the leaps.

Triple Jump in the arena

At first glance, the Triple Jump might appear complicated, but its rules are relatively simple and very similar to those of the Long Jump – its close cousin in the world of horizontal jumps.

Arena Facts

The runway is usually parallel to one of the straights of the track and is 1.22 metres long. The distance between the take-off board and the far end of the landing area for men should be at least 21m. For international meetings, the take-off line should be not less than 13m for men and 11m for women from the nearer end of the landing area.

Plasticine is often placed in front of the board to help officials tell whether the attempt was illegal.

Triple Jump is a dynamic event and the action of the hop, step and jump is physically demanding.

The landing area is between 2.75m and 3m and is filled with sand, with the top of it level with the take-off board. After each jump, the sand is smoothed over with a rake by officials.

Jumping

The rules are almost identical to the Long Jump. The main difference is that the take-off board has to be further away in order for the hop and step phases to be completed.

Athletes are not allowed to place markers on the runway to remind them where their run-up begins, but they are able to place markers at the side of the runway.

When hopping, the athlete lands first on the same foot as that from which they have taken off. In the step, the athlete lands on the opposite foot. But the whole jump is not judged a failure if the athlete touches the ground with their 'sleeping leg'.

Athletes can jump from as far behind the take-off board – or foul line – as they wish, but the distance measured is from the board to the nearest

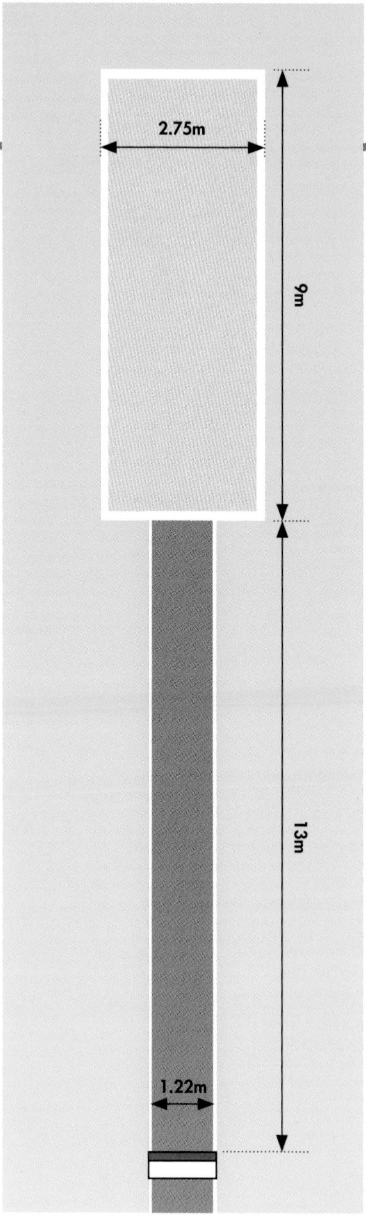

2.75m

9m

13m

1.22m

mark made in the sand that is closest to the board. If the athlete touches the ground beyond the take-off board, the jump is judged to be a foul.

Athletes usually have three jumps and their best effort is the one that counts. In some competitions the best athletes go forward into what is effectively a second round of jumps, with a further three attempts. If this happens, the best mark in all six rounds wins.

Wind speeds are often taken and if the speed during a jump is measured at greater than 2m per second the jump will be allowed to stand in the competition but will not be accepted for record purposes.

On landing, athletes must exit the sandpit and not walk back through it. If they do, they will leave a mark close to the take-off board that will be the one used for measuring.

Key Rules

- The athlete must complete a hop, step and jump – in that order.
- The distance measured is from the take-off board to the part of the mark in the sand that is nearest the board.
- If an athlete jumps from beyond the take-off board, it is a foul.

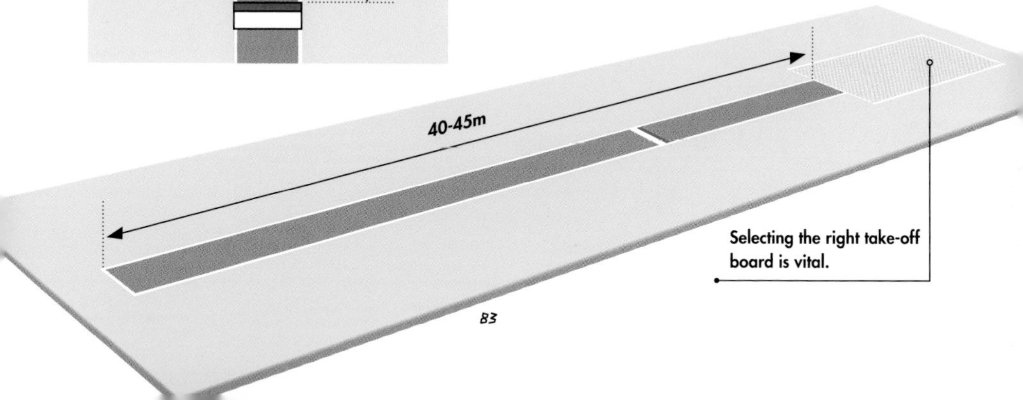

40-45m

Selecting the right take-off board is vital.

Triple Jump techniques explained

Triple Jump technique can be split into several sections and here we look at the approach run, take off and the hop phases of the event.

Unlike the Long Jump, the seemingly more complicated Triple Jump has one standard technique that is universally used. This can be broken down into four phases – the approach run and take-off, the hop, the step and the jump.

Approach run and take-off

The approach run is similar to that in the Long Jump, but generally not quite as fast. At the start of the run-up the athlete accelerates and leans forward slightly. During this mid-phase, speed reaches a high level and the athlete begins to run more upright. Then, as the athlete reaches the take-off board, the leg speed reaches its peak and the athlete maintains good form.

Athletes usually need around 18–20 strides during their run-up, with faster athletes often requiring more. Younger athletes, however, will often reach top speed early during the approach – and therefore need a shorter run-up, with the number of strides ideally matching their age.

The start of the approach run should be marked and made from a standing start to ensure consistency. Windy conditions may also affect the run-up.

The number of strides in Triple Jump should roughly match your age.

Midway through the hop, the take-off leg will be pointing forward and high.

At take-off, the triple jumper aims to go through the air more horizontally than the long jumper. The hips of a triple jumper are also further forward.

Hop

After a low take-off, the athlete drives the thigh of the (non-jumping) leg and then swings it backward. As this happens, the thigh of the jumping leg rises, leading to a position mid-hop where the knee of the jumping leg is pointing forward and high, and the non-jumping leg is at the rear.

The jumping leg hits the ground in a 'clawing' action and flexes at the knee as it prepares to rebound into the step phase. The arms work hard to keep the body as balanced as possible.

Some athletes try to hop too high, but this is an error as they will often collapse at the end of this phase and be left with little momentum for the step and jump that follow. A shorter penultimate stride and leaning forward slightly at take-off will sometimes solve this problem.

Technique Tips

- Keep your hop low in order to conserve horizontal velocity.
- Maintain an erect body position during the phases.
- Try to have a 'pawing' or 'clutching' action with the legs through the hop and step landings.
- Save energy for the final jump phase.

The foot hits the ground with a clawing action and the knee slightly bent.

Maintain form and balance as you enter the step phase.

Triple Jump techniques explained

The run-up, take-off and hop completed, now it is time to look at the final stages of the Triple Jump – the step and the jump phases.

Step

This is often the shortest phase of the Triple Jump and great effort should be made to maintain form and balance. The leading leg thrusts forward, so that in the midpoint of this phase there is once again a large gap between both feet. The foot should extend backward, forming an angle of almost 90 degrees. Meanwhile, the take-off foot must extend forward, making an angle greater than 90 degrees. Then, as the shin is extended, the ankle should become locked.

Be careful not to land on the ball of the foot, as it is sometimes a temptation to overreach with the toes for distance instead of making sure you land flat-footed. Try to develop a feel for the ground as you 'claw' or 'paw' backward and feel the ground drag backward underneath your body.

If the whole jump has collapsed by this stage and the step phase is too short, then the athlete might need to gain more strength with repeat bounding drills. Powerful arm action and driving the thigh of the leading leg can also assist.

Jump

All of the athlete's aggression should be put into this final phase as the foot – which is usually, but not always, different

Try to land flat-footed and not on the ball of the foot.

During the step phase there is a large gap between the feet.

from the Long Jump take-off foot – pushes off. The athlete will aim for good distance and a solid landing position with the feet well ahead of the rest of the body.

The simplest approach is for the knees to be tucked up to the chest as much as is possible – similar to the 'sail' technique used by beginners in the Long Jump (see pages 76–7).

Alternatively, more experienced athletes use a 'hang' technique, where the legs trail the body before being brought forward at the last moment before landing (see pages 76–7).

If the jump phase is very weak compared to other phases, try to

maintain good horizontal speed throughout the whole jump and practise doing Long Jump efforts but with a take-off from your non-favoured leg.

Like Long Jump, try not to fall back into the sand either, as judges will measure from the mark nearest the take-off board.

Arm Action
A double-arm action is used by many elite triple jumpers. The alternating arm action feels more natural to many athletes – and is therefore ideal for beginners.

Technique Tips
- Maximise your speed on the take-off.
- Keep the distance of the hop, step and jump as equal as possible.
- Try to have a 'pawing' or 'clutching' action with the legs through the hop and step landings.
- Try not to jump too high in the hop and step. Save energy for the final jump.

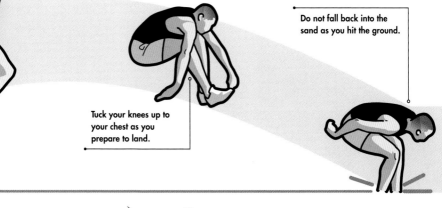

Use the arms in this final stage of the Triple Jump.

Tuck your knees up to your chest as you prepare to land.

Do not fall back into the sand as you hit the ground.

Triple Jump training tips and techniques

Triple Jump training is demanding and includes many elements, but the most important is probably rebound jumping, as this is hugely specific to the main event itself.

Early Training

If you are young or new to the Triple Jump, it is wise to limit the amount of bounding during the early stages. Instead, it is recommended to gradually build up the resilience of your body with strength and conditioning training. Light bounding on cushioned surfaces is also good.

Generally, Triple Jump training involves gym and weights work, plus sprint drills and some endurance work. Strength exercises might include clean and jerk, single-leg squats and lunges, while circuit training is also useful. The type of training that is most specific to this field event, however, is 'rebound jumping'.

Rebound Jumping

This kind of training is vital for a triple jumper and involves drills where you hit the ground and then immediately bounce back again – like a ball. Muscles undergo a lengthening contraction during landing and an explosive shortening contraction of the same muscles during take-off – just what the body needs to do in the Triple Jump competition itself.

Safety While Rebound Jumping

- Flex your knees in order to help absorb shock.
- Land on the full foot, not the heel or ball.
- Roll off the foot as you push forward during the rebound action.

Bounding exercises are a major part of Triple Jump training.

Land on your whole foot, not the ball or heel.

Try to use cushioned surfaces when doing this kind of work.

Training Tips

- Practise doing a hop, step and jump from a standing start. This will get the body used to the movement but with less risk of injury and no need to worry about speed and hitting a take-off board.
- Uphill bounding can increase your leg strength.
- Single-leg hops up stairs or one-legged hops with a butt kick action are good for developing the hop phase. Also, practise hopping with the knee coming up high.

- To practise the step phase, set the take-off board so that you end up in the sandpit after the step. Then do a run-up, hop and step, but no jump.
- For a better final jump phase, use a short run-up of six strides and then just step and jump into the sand, with no hop phase. Go for a dynamic final leap, aiming for height in this last part of the Triple Jump.

Common Faults

- If you struggle to hit the take-off board, then try using a larger take-off zone (see page 78).
- If a problem occurs in a certain part of the Triple Jump, the cause often lies with improper technique in the previous phase.
- If you hop too high you will be left with little momentum for the step and jump that follow. A shorter penultimate stride and leaning forward slightly at take-off will sometimes solve this problem.
- If your jump phase is very weak compared to other phases, try to maintain good horizontal speed throughout the whole jump and practise Long Jump efforts but with a take-off from your non-favoured leg.

If you have a problem in part of the jump, poor technique is usually to blame.

Shot Put

Among the giants of the athletics arena, shot putters display huge strength, but only athletes with great technical ability will truly shine on the big stage.

Olympic History

The Shot Put was not favoured by the Ancient Greeks, who instead preferred the more aesthetically pleasing Javelin and Discus throws. But it is nonetheless an established event in the modern Olympic Games, and at the Athens 2004 Games it was given its own stage when the medals were fought over at the ancient site of Olympia.

In recent centuries, the event has developed from the stone-throwing competitions favoured by sportsmen from countries such as Scotland. Indeed, the Scottish 'stone' weighs slightly more than a modern-day shot and it is where the origins of the modern implement are to be found.

Ideal Physical Qualities

Shot putters are among the strongmen of track and field, although speed and general athleticism are also vital in order to move across the small throwing circle while being careful not to fall out of its perimeter.

Clothing and Footwear

Specialist shoes allow the thrower to move across the circle and provide good stability. Pick your footwear carefully, though, as shoes are made separately

Reese Hoffa

Reese Hoffa is one of several American men who have won world or Olympic titles in recent years. Hoffa has not won Olympic gold, but he has taken world indoor and outdoor crowns and is one of the most charismatic athletes in any track and field event.

Standing at just under 6 feet tall, Hoffa uses the spin technique to generate speed in the circle. Outside Shot Put, he is adept at throwing other objects around too – he is a skilled juggler and can solve the Rubik's Cube in half a minute.

34.92°

2.135m

75cm

The Shot Put landing area fans out at close to 35 degrees from the throwing circle.

Shot putters wear specialist footwear with smooth soles to assist them when moving in the throwing circle.

A 10cm high stop board marks the front of the Shot Put circle.

Athletes must be careful not step out of the throwing circle.

for the glide and spin techniques.

The spin technique requires a shoe that is smooth on the bottom with a rounded sole. Shoes for gliders, on the other hand, offer a flat sole and are less smooth. Not surprisingly, as the throwing surface is concrete, spiked shoes are not allowed.

Singlet and shorts are worn in competitions and athletes may also use chalk on their hands and necks to improve their grip.

Key Rules
- The shot must be held in one hand close to the chin and cannot move behind the line of the shoulders as it is pushed away from the body.
- Throwers can only touch the inner side of the stop board.

Standards to Aspire to

	Senior	U20	U17	U15	U13
Men	10.00m (7.26kg)	10.00m (6kg)	10.00m (5kg)	9.50m (4kg)	6.50m (3.25kg)
Women	8.30m (4kg)	7.60m (4kg)	7.25m (4kg)	7.40m (3.25m)	6.00m (2.72kg)

Shot Put in the arena

An event that combines brute strength with skilful technique, the Shot Put sees the athlete "putting", or throwing in a pushing action, a heavy metal ball as far as possible.

The Shot

The shot, which is smooth and made out of iron or brass, is thrown on to grass or something that will leave an imprint.

The weight of the shot varies according to age and gender (see page opposite).

Athletes cannot make use of anything to help them throw, such as gloves or taping their fingers together (although some taping is allowed if approved by officials). Substances such as chalk are allowed for a better grip of the shot, though, and this can also be placed on the neck.

Arena Facts

The inside of the throwing circle is just over 2 metres in diameter and made of concrete or another firm but not slippery surface. A stop board sits at the end of the circle. It is about 10 centimetres high, coloured white and in the shape of an arc.

Throwing

The shot itself has to be 'put' from the shoulder with one hand only. The shot touches, or is very close, to the neck or chin and should not be dropped below this position during the action of putting. The shot should also not be taken behind the line of the shoulders.

The athlete can touch the inner rim of the stop board, but cannot touch the top or step over it, and must leave the back half

of the circle after each throw. The shot must also land within the sector lines.

If no rule has been broken, then the thrower is entitled to abort an attempt halfway through, then retake the throw – all within a one-minute time limit.

Measurements are made straight after each throw and athletes typically have between three and six attempts to make their best throw.

Safety

Given the weight of the shot, safety is an important issue. Inexperienced athletes will be prone to accidents, especially when trying the spin technique, as the shot can fall loose due to centrifugal force pulling it away from the body.

In competitions or training, never throw

the shot around apart from when in the circle making a genuine competitive or training effort.

Weight of Shots

	Senior	U20	U17	U15	U13
Men	7.26kg	6kg	5kg	4kg	3.25kg
Women	4kg	4kg	4kg	3.25kg	2.72kg

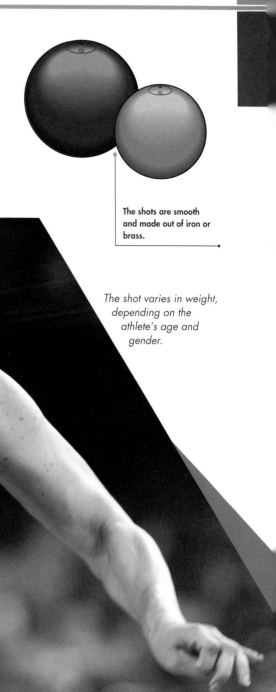

The shots are smooth and made out of iron or brass.

The shot varies in weight, depending on the athlete's age and gender.

Shot Put techniques explained

There are two main techniques in the Shot Put – the glide (or linear) method and the spin (or rotational) style. Bigger, heavier throwers often adopt the glide technique, while shorter, faster athletes become spinners.

Spinners rotate around the circle in a similar fashion to discus throwers, while gliders, as the name suggests, glide across before pushing the shot powerfully into the air. Generally, the spin is favoured to give slightly more chance of a bigger distance, but it is more unpredictable and spinners can be inconsistent as a result. Ultimately, it is down to personal preference.

The men's world record is held by a spinner, but the No. 2 all-time and women's world record-holder are gliders.

Holding the Shot

Hold the implement in your non-throwing hand. Now hold the fingers of your throwing hand loosely, with the thumb out, and slap them on to the top of the shot. Roll the shot over into your throwing hand and the weight should rest across the ridge of your hand between fingers and palm. The position of the shot on your neck is one of personal preference.

Glide Technique

Athletes stand at the back of the circle with their backs facing the direction of where the shot will be thrown. For a right-handed thrower, weight is usually put on the right leg, which is flexed slightly as the other leg points backward. The left arm is held in a relaxed fashion.

After making a small and low hop towards the front of the circle, the athlete turns side-on and prepares to throw. The body will then twist as the legs, arms and

Stand at the back of the circle with your back facing the direction of the throw.

Prepare to make a low and small hop to the centre of the circle.

Keep your weight on your right leg and your left arm relaxed. Twist your body as you turn side-on and prepare to throw.

Related to the throwing style used in Discus, the spin technique requires good balance, but superb distances can be achieved with this method.

body work together to apply as much force as possible and the shot is released from a high position.

The technique was developed by Parry O'Brien, the 1952 and 1956 Olympic Games champion from the United States.

Spin Technique
This method of throwing is related to the style used in the Discus Throw. For a right-handed athlete, the body rotates around the left foot, travelling from the back of the circle to the front.

The shoulders and shot are turned fully to the right rear before rotating across the circle. The action has to be tight

and controlled due to the small size of the circle. The legs rotate ahead of the shoulders.

The shot itself can also move away from the neck during the turn, due to centrifugal force, unless it is pushed in against the athlete until the moment it is thrown.

Technique Tips
- The idea with both glide and spin techniques is to release the shot with maximum velocity.
- Aim to put the shot at an angle of about 40 degrees.
- Cradle the shot firmly under the chin and push it away with a powerful thrust.
- When spinning, rotate on the balls of your feet.

Push the ball from your chin as your whole body works in synchrony.

The thrower can make contact with the stop board but they must be careful not to step out of the throwing circle.

Shot Put training tips and techniques

Whichever of the two popular techniques you choose – the glide or the spin – there are plenty of exercises and drills you can do to improve the distance you achieve.

General weights and gym work aside, you will improve in throwing the shot if you carry out specialist throwing drills. Here are some popular ones.

Standing Throw

Learning to put the shot from a standing position is excellent practice and mastering this will help later progression on to the glide or spin techniques.

Like the full glide technique, put most weight on your right foot (if you are right-handed) and face away from the direction of throw with the shot under your chin. Bend the right leg and reach back with the left.

Lower your upper body, then push upward and rotate 180 degrees as you

straighten your legs and push your chest and hips forward. Power your arm and snap your fingers as the ball is released.

Medicine Ball Throw

Push a medicine ball vigorously from under your chin from a standing start. Place a bar – perhaps on High Jump standards – and aim to get the ball over the bar to a training partner on the other side. If you manage it, take a pace backward and try again.

Seated Throw

Sit in a firm chair that can support your weight properly. Then, focusing on good technique, with a high elbow, thrust the shot from under your chin. The exercise builds power and helps the final pushing phase of the Shot Put.

Rear Overhead Throw

An enjoyable drill where the thrower holds the shot in both hands and with legs shoulder-width apart goes into a squatting position.

Men's Shot Put was contested at the first Modern Olympic Games in Athens in 1896 and the women's in London in 1948.

Hold the shot out in front of you with both arms while squatting, but then bring it down between your legs before thrusting upward with the legs while simultaneously swinging the arms over the head and releasing the shot into the air. Naturally, be ultra-cautious when attempting this drill.

Wrist Flip

Start with the shot overhead in your throwing hand, then flip the shot out of your hand into the throwing sector. This promotes proper release of the shot.

Strapped Arm Throw

Use a bandage to strap the forearm of your throwing arm to underneath the armpit of your non-throwing arm. Then carry out a normal Shot Put technique minus the final push at the end. You will learn how important using your body is – and it will need to be used well if the shot is not to drop on your toes!

Common Faults and Remedies

- If there is no thrust from the fingers, your handhold may be wrong. Try pushing from the palm not the fingers and practise standing puts using light shots.
- In the glide, to avoid a large and high hop across the circle, glide close to the ground.
- When spinning, if you lose control of the shot and it lands outside the sector then practise slow rotations using a light shot or even no shot.

Discus Throw

From the days of Ancient Greece to the modern London 2012 Olympic Games and Paralympic Games, the Discus has endured throughout the ages and is a symbol of the speed, strength and skill required to excel in Athletics.

Olympic History

The sight of a man throwing a discus is one of the classic images in Athletics. One of the original events in the Ancient Greek Olympic Games, the Discus has since featured on the official posters and stamps for several of the modern Games. Of these, the most enduring image is that of Myron's statue *Discobolus*, which shows a naked man carrying a discus.

Athletes at the ancient Olympic Games threw from a straight run-up, similar to the modern-day Javelin. The early modern Games then featured standing and freestyle techniques before today's method of turning in the circle became established.

Overall, the Discus is one of the most aesthetically pleasing Athletics events, and this is due partly to the aerodynamic nature of the discus itself. One of the quirks of the sport is that ideal conditions involve throwing into a slight headwind.

Ideal Physical Qualities

The Discus requires both power and grace as athletes spin in the circle before unleashing the discus out into the in-field. Athletes who excel at throwing the discus are usually large, strong individuals but also have the speed and flexibility to move around the circle.

Above all, balance is the key ingredient in good discus throwing and the best in the

Al Oerter

A US sporting legend, Al Oerter won the Olympic Discus title at the Melbourne 1956, Rome 1960, Tokyo 1964 and Mexico 1968 Games.

During his final Games triumph, in Mexico, he was not favourite to win, but produced an Olympic record of 64.78m to take gold and become the first-ever track and field athlete to win a title at four consecutive Olympic Games.

Later, he tried to make the Olympic team in 1980 aged 44, but finished fourth in the US trials.

world can hurl a 2-kilogram discus further than 70 metres. It is also an event that requires many years of practice – both of a technical nature and building strength in the weights room. Therefore most throwers do not reach their peak until they are in their 30s.

Clothing and Footwear

Specialist footwear is worn to allow the thrower to spin around the circle. Shoes are often made for use in both the Discus and the Hammer due to the similar circular range of motion employed by the athlete. Singlet and shorts are standard clothes, while discus throwers often use chalk to improve their grip.

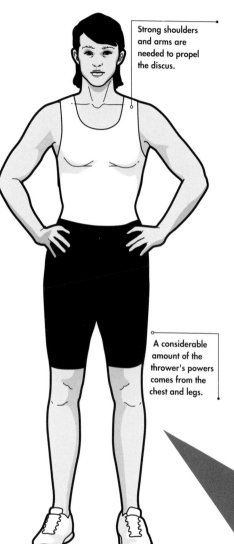

Strong shoulders and arms are needed to propel the discus.

A considerable amount of the thrower's powers comes from the chest and legs.

Specialist shoes with smooth soles help the discus thrower rotate in the throwing circle.

Standards to Aspire to

	Senior	U20	U17	U15	U13
Men	28.00m (2kg)	25.00m (1.75kg)	25.00m (1.5kg)	23.00m (1.25kg)	14.00m (1kg)
Women	25.00m (1kg)	23.00m (1kg)	21.00m (1kg)	18.00m (1kg)	13.00m (0.75kg)

Discus Throw in the arena

Like caged animals, discus throwers pace backward and forward before releasing their implement into the in-field. The netting that surrounds the athlete is necessary for everyone's safety, though, in this dangerous event.

The Discus

The discus is made from wood, or a similarly suitable material, with a smooth metal rim. The size varies according to the age of the athlete – for men it is 22 centimetres in diameter and 2 kilograms in weight, while for women it is 18cm and 1kg.

Taping or gloves cannot be used to help hold the discus, but chalk or a similar substance can be used to help grip.

Arena Facts

The diameter of the throwing circle – at 2.5 metres – is a little bigger than the circle for the Shot Put and Hammer Throw. It has a concrete or similar surface.

For international competition, the mouth of the cage is 6m wide and is 7m in front of the centre of the throwing circle. The netting panels should be at least 4m at their lowest point and the nets should never be closer than 3m to the centre of the circle.

Throwing

At the start of the throw the athlete must be stationary. As with all throws, the implement must land within the sector lines. Athletes must not step over the front of the circle during the throw and must also leave the circle from the back behind the line in the centre of the circle,

otherwise a foul throw will be given. The athlete also has to remain in the circle until the discus has landed.

Between three and six attempts are allowed, depending on the type of competition, and the distance is measured from the nearest mark made by the discus to the inside of the circumference of the circle along a line to the centre of the circle.

It is not a failure, however, if the discus hits the cage, provided that no other rules are broken. Athletes can also stop their attempt, leave the circle and start again if no other infringements have been made.

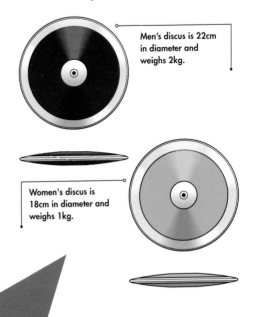

Men's discus is 22cm in diameter and weighs 2kg.

Women's discus is 18cm in diameter and weighs 1kg.

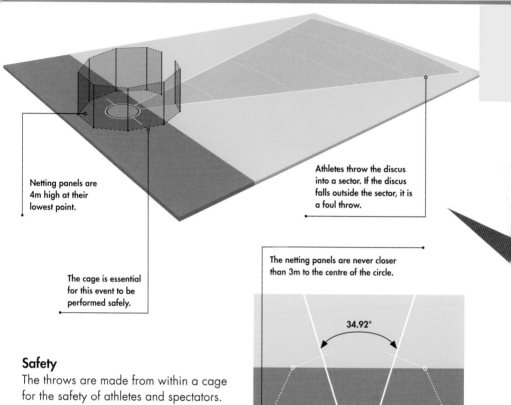

Netting panels are 4m high at their lowest point.

Athletes throw the discus into a sector. If the discus falls outside the sector, it is a foul throw.

The cage is essential for this event to be performed safely.

The netting panels are never closer than 3m to the centre of the circle.

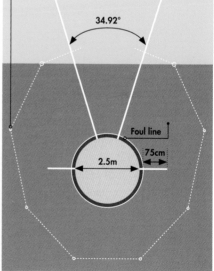

Safety

The throws are made from within a cage for the safety of athletes and spectators. The cages are made so that they stop a 2kg discus that is flying at 25 metres per second. Such is their design that they prevent the discus from rebounding back at the athlete, too.

Key Rules

- Circle infringements, such as stepping out of the circle during the throw, or not leaving via the back half of the circle after the attempt, will be judged a foul.
- The athlete with the longest throw is the winner and ties are decided by determining which athlete has the longer second-best throw.

Discus Throw techniques explained

Despite the complex turn during the throw, the technique in the Discus Thow is universally recognised and there are barely any variations on the accepted best method. But Discus throwers must have the strength of a bear and the balance of a ballet dancer if they want to reach their potential.

Holding the Discus

First, place your left hand under the discus and your right hand on top (if you are right-handed). Spread your fingers very slightly, being careful not to overstretch them, with the first joint of the fingers curling over the rim.

Do not grip the discus hard, but instead allow it to rest on this first joint of the fingers, with the tips just over the rim. The first two fingers should be pretty close, with the others around 5–10 millimetres apart from each other and the wrist slightly flexed.

When holding a Discus, spread your fingers very slightly, being careful not to overstretch them. The first two fingers should be close, with the others 5–10mm apart.

Technique

Like the spin technique in Shot Put, discus throwers start facing 180 degrees away from the landing area and rotate around their feet before releasing the discus.

Do not grip the Discuss too hard and allow it to rest on the first joint of the fingers.

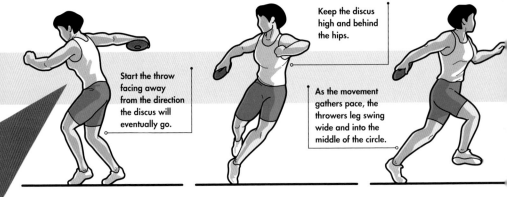

Start the throw facing away from the direction the discus will eventually go.

Keep the discus high and behind the hips.

As the movement gathers pace, the throwers leg swing wide and into the middle of the circle.

Asssumming a straddle-like stance with feet more than shoulder-width apart, the athlete begins by making preliminary – and long – swings, often called the 'wind-up'. The weight is kept over the middle of the stance and the rhythm involves the discus swinging around and across the body.

For a right-handed thrower, the left foot is then turned around, and as the right foot leaves the ground the weight is placed over the left leg. Throughout, the discus is kept high and behind the hips.

As the movement gathers pace, the right leg swings wide and into the middle of the circle. On hitting the ground, the right foot pivots on the ball of the foot and, ideally, the knee and chin should sit above the toes on this right foot.

Having left its original position at the back, the left foot swings around and eventually hits the ground at the front. As this happens, the left arm points in the direction of the throw and the right foot pivots while the right hip drives forward.

The right arm, meanwhile, stays relaxed and ready to unleash the discus. Finally, as the left side of the body stops quite suddenly, the right arm comes through fast to release at an angle of around 35 degrees. The discus is spun off the index finger or the middle finger.

The best throwers learn to move through this sequence at high speed, while maintaining balance and releasing the discus with power at the end.

Technical Options

- Some throwers swing the right leg with a wide action before quickly folding it as it comes into the centre of the circle.
- It is also possible to make an initial turn on the heel of the left foot, before rolling on to the toe – a difficult manoeuvre that needs good balance.
- When the discus is thrown, some athletes prefer to keep both feet grounded, whereas others like to drive vertically, thus causing the feet to leave the floor.

As the left side of the body stops, the right arm comes through fast to release the discus at a 35-degree angle.

As the right foot hits the centre of the circle, it pivots on the ball of the foot.

Stay balanced as you spin in the circle with speed.

Break the Discus technique down into a series of stages and drills before you put it all together in the competition itself by delivering one smooth and rhythmic throw.

Read the correct technique for the Discus and you may be left with the impression that it is a series of staccato movements. In fact, the Discus requires the athlete to move from stage to stage with rhythm and great synchrony. However, when doing technical training work, many drills focus on practising one part of the throw before you try to put all the stages together. They include:

Starting Drill

Begin in the starting position, with your left foot at the centre back of the circle and feet more than shoulder-width apart. Your weight should also be on the left foot.

With practice, weight can be shifted from left to right during the wind-up stage, helping you to gain momentum before the full rotation begins. You will also gain a feel for centrifugal force.

Standing Throw

Practising this will help you to learn how to control the discus as it is released at an ideal angle of about 35 degrees.

Walking Turn

Practise this to get used to turning. Step with the left foot and then step with the right foot underneath the body. Do a reverse pivot on the right foot, before walking for a couple of steps, and then do another turn.

Throws for Height

In order to promote proper release of the discus, stand with your feet shoulder-width apart, swing the discus to and fro twice in front of your body and then throw it up high, ensuring the throwing arm is straight.

Reversing and Non-reversing

One slight technical difference is that some throwers reverse their feet when releasing the discus. In other words, their left foot is forward when the discus is thrown but the force of the throw causes the right foot to swing forward in front of the left. The alternative technique, of course, is a non-reverse throw, where this does not happen.

Time to Shape Up

One good training tip is to use a clock analogy when discussing the various points of the circle. Imagine 6 o'clock is the front and centre of the circle, for example, where the discus will be released from, while the back and middle of the circle is 12 o'clock.

Don't Forget

Technical work aside, much of a discus thrower's ability comes from developing strength and speed in the gym. Weight training, plyometrics, sprinting

and mobility work will all help you to make the most of your potential.

Throwing the discus, however, is not as physically taxing as, say, the javelin, so it is possible to throw four or five times a week.

Common Faults and Remedies

- Using your shoulders to initiate the turn is incorrect. Use your legs and feet instead.
- If the thrower loses balance, put more body weight over the left foot at the start of the turn.

Practising your technique in a series of drills will help you to deliver a smooth throw in competition.

Hammer Throw

Like their cousins on the Highland Games circuit, Hammer throwers show impressive power, speed, mobility and technical finesse as they throw their implement high into the sky.

Olympic History

The origins of the Hammer Throw can be traced back to Scotland and Ireland. Even today, similar Throwing events are part of the Highland Games. Originally, a heavy sledge was thrown. More recent Highland Games have seen a heavy ball attached to a rigid wooden stick hurled.

In the Modern Olympic Games, the Hammer has been an established event for men for more than a century. But for women it has only recently entered major competitions, making its Olympic debut in the Sydney 2000 Games.

Ideal Physical Qualities

Hammer athletes are strong, fast, skilful and dynamic as they spin in the circle, getting faster with every turn,

before letting go with perfect timing. Initially, during the early 1900s, it was a strongman's event. But gradually technique began to improve during the 1950s and 1960s and then the Soviet Union throwers really began to improve on the world record during the 1970s as they perfected the technique of turning quickly in the circle to get the hammer at maximum speed before it is released.

Top athletes can hurl the hammer out to distances of 70–80 metres. It takes years

Yuriy Sedykh

Yuriy Sedykh won the Olympic Hammer Throw title at the 1976 Montreal and 1980 Moscow Games and he set the world record of 86.74m when he took one of three European titles during the late 1970s and 1980s.

The former Soviet athlete is widely regarded as the greatest Hammer thrower in history and, unusually, he threw off only three turns as opposed to four.

He lives in France with his wife, Natalya Lisovskaya, the world record-holder and 1988 Olympic champion in the Shot Put.

of practice, however, and throwers usually reach their peak after literally tens of thousands of throws in training.

Clothing and Footwear

When it comes to footwear, the same shoes can be worn as in the Discus, as a similar turning action on a concrete surface is carried out. Traditional singlet and shorts complete the athletics apparel. Gloves are also allowed in this event.

As well as supreme upper body strength, athletes must have excellent rotational speed and balance.

Typical Discus event clothing consists of a vest and shorts, leggings or singlet. Support belts can also be worn.

Discus shoes have a smooth sole to ensure maximum contact with the throwing circle.

Standards to Aspire to

	Senior	U20	U17	U15	U13
Men	26.00m (7.26kg)	25.00m (6kg)	24.00m (5kg)	23.00m (4kg)	–
Women	25.00m (4kg)	23.00m (4kg)	19.00m (4kg)	21.00m (3.25kg)	–

Hammer Throw in the arena

The obvious dangers aside, the Hammer is a beautiful event when perfectly executed. Rhythmic turns build to a crescendo of speed until the ball and wire are unleashed, travelling extraordinary distances.

The Hammer

The hammer itself is made of a metal head (iron or brass and sometimes filled with lead), plus a spring steel wire and a rigid handle that does not have any hinged joints.

The weight of the hammer varies depending on the age and gender of the athlete (see chart on page 107) and the length also differs slightly, but is generally around 1.2 metres.

Arena Facts

The Hammer uses facilities similar to the Shot Put and Discus Throw. The throwing circle is the same size as the one used for the Shot Put, but it does not have a stop board. The circle, as in Discus, is surrounded by netting for safety purposes – this is basically because the discus and hammer fly much further than the shot and also have the potential to veer off in different directions.

This cage should be capable of stopping a 7.26-kilogram hammer moving at speeds of at least 32m per second. The mouth of the cage, through which the hammer is thrown, is 6m wide and 7m in distance in front of the centre of the circle.

The netting for international competition is at least 7m high at the rear and 10m high on the panels closest to the mouth. Two of these panels near the mouth are movable, too, and one of them can be opened by an official, depending on whether a right or left-handed thrower is about to make an attempt.

Throwing

Like other throws, in the Hammer athletes can abort an attempt partway through and start again, as long as no other rules have been broken. Hammer

Hammers have the potential to be a lethal weapon, so throwers should not practise alone or without supervision.

The Hammer consists of a metal head and a spring steel wire and a rigid handle.

The mouth of the cage is 6m wide. The hammer is a lethal weapon, so a well-made cage is crucial.

Hammers can travel a long way, so officials must be alert at all times.

throwers can even stop and gather themselves mid-throw by swinging the hammer and passing it from hand to hand. They have one minute to complete an entire throw, however.

The hammer head can touch the ground anywhere before and during the throw.

Three to six attempts are allowed, depending on the type of competition.

Safety

Obviously a flying hammer can be dangerous, so throwers should not practise alone or without supervision from a coach. Horns are blown during competitions to alert other athletes that a throw is being made.

The cage should be capable of stopping a 7.26-kilogram Hammer travelling at speeds of 32m per second.

Key Rules

- The head of the hammer can be placed on the ground inside or outside the circle at the start of the throw.
- There is no penalty if the hammer hits the ground during the throw.

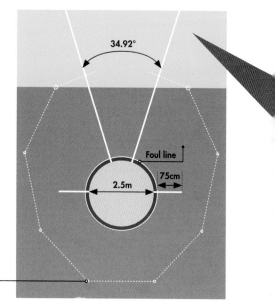

34.92°

Foul line

75cm

2.5m

Hammer Throw techniques explained

Elite hammer throwers are a blur of speed as they turn in the circle. Yet the technique can be broken down into smaller parts to be practised separately before putting them together as a whole.

Hammer technique can be split into two main areas – the pre-spin and then the turns themselves and delivery.

Preliminary Spin

Athletes stand with their backs to the landing sector, with the upper body turned a little to the right and, for right-handed throwers, the hammer behind to the right-hand side. Athletes will also be at the back of the circle with their feet shoulder-width apart.

As the hammer swings upward, the athlete's arms bend so that the hands pass near the forehead. The thrower ducks under the hammer as it accelerates and moves from its high point at the left rear of the thrower to the low point at the right front. The arms then straighten as

the hammer drops back to its low point to the thrower's right.

Turns and Delivery

After two or three preliminary spins, the athlete is ready to start moving across the circle. The thrower moves with the hammer, pivoting on the heel of the left foot and completing on the ball of the foot.

As the athlete pivots on the left foot, the right foot leaves the ground and moves with the thrower during the second half of the turn. It is possible to make three or four turns, but if four turns are attempted, then the first must be done on the toe of the left foot alone, otherwise the thrower will run out of space. The idea is also to make each turn slightly faster than the last, as the

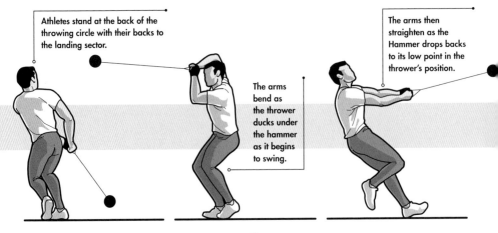

Athletes stand at the back of the throwing circle with their backs to the landing sector.

The arms bend as the thrower ducks under the hammer as it begins to swing.

The arms then straighten as the Hammer drops backs to its low point in the thrower's position.

hammer picks up velocity.

Alternatively, beginners can use one or two pre-swings followed by just one or two turns. In competitions, very inexperienced athletes are even allowed to throw with pre-spins only and no turns whatsoever if they wish.

During the delivery of the hammer, the right foot is placed down at the end of the final turn and the body extends as the hammer is pulled up by lifting the chest and straightening the legs and back with a powerful movement. When the hammer is released, the body is fully extended, with the left shoulder pointing towards the direction of throw.

Finally, without stepping on or over the rim of the circle, the athlete rotates on the right foot and brings the left foot to the rear.

Technique Tips

- During the pre-spins, do not let your left shoulder move backward.
- The hammer should remain low at the back of the circle and high at the front as you turn. The optimum angle of release is 45 degrees.
- Use wooden sticks or similar items during practice in order to get used to the necessary footwork.

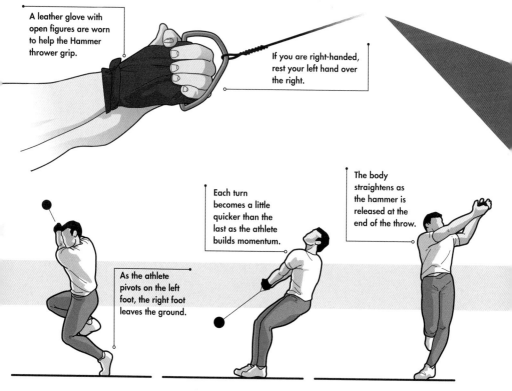

A leather glove with open figures are worn to help the Hammer thrower grip.

If you are right-handed, rest your left hand over the right.

Each turn becomes a little quicker than the last as the athlete builds momentum.

The body straightens as the hammer is released at the end of the throw.

As the athlete pivots on the left foot, the right foot leaves the ground.

Hammer Throw training techniques

Due to safety reasons – and also to minimise the chances of injury and wear and tear on the body – many parts of the Hammer technique can be practised by using light wooden poles or balls.

Speed and balance are of the essence. The faster you can get your feet around and down on the ground ahead of your torso and the hammer during the turn, the better you will be able to accelerate the hammer towards its high point and down to its low point. Here are three drills that can help with the swing, turn and release.

Swings Using Light Implements

Using a broom handle or pole that is just over a metre long, extend both arms and hold the pole with your right hand just beyond the left (if you are right-handed). Pull the hammer upward to the left and with the legs slightly bent rotate your shoulders to the right and bring the pole to its low point on the right side.

Using a football or basketball in a net makes a great – and very safe – substitute for a hammer and this drill can also be done using one of these makeshift devices.

Turns Using Light Implements

Again, as with the swings, use a pole, football or basketball as you practise the turning movement. Look forward at all times and keep a balanced squatting position. Complete a full 180-degree rotation on your left heel and keep your arms extended and the knees close together during the turn.

Medicine Ball Throw

This can be done in several ways and helps simulate the delivery of the hammer at the end of the throw. Either squat down, hold the ball with both hands between your legs and then rise on to your toes and throw the ball in a scooping motion as high as you can. Or stand up, then bend over and hold the ball with both hands between your legs, rise again and throw the ball backward as powerfully as possible. This final drill can be done by throwing backward against a wall and then turning to catch the ball as it rebounds.

Finally, put the swing, turn and throw together into one movement. In addition to practising technique, you can build strength in the weights room and gym. Mobility exercises are also important due to the fast turning action that needs to be done in the circle.

Safety While Training

- The hammer is dangerous. Use a wooden stick or ball in a net when practising foot movements.
- Always throw within a cage – beginners can easily let go at the wrong moment or lose control of the hammer.
- Take care in wet conditions.

Common Faults and Remedies

- If you lose balance, make sure your legs are flexed and you are looking forward. Practise with a pole, too.
- Flexing the arms during the throw can be a sign of nervousness. Imagine the hammer is an extension of your arms.

Technique, strength and mobility exercises are the key to Hammer success.

Javelin Throw

The Javelin Throw is one of the most glamorous and attractive events in the athletics world. Part of its charm is its rich history, which dates back to the dawn of time itself.

Olympic History

The Javelin is probably the oldest of all field events. Its origins, after all, lie in hunting and warfare, as the javelin itself is basically a type of spear. The event has changed considerably over the years – in the Ancient Greek Olympic Games, a leather thong was wrapped around the middle of the javelin, making It spiral in the air, while modern variations have included a two-handed contest, with the Javelin thrown with both hands separately and the marks added together.

The javelin itself has also changed in recent years. When Uwe Hohn of East Germany threw the javelin an incredible distance of 104.80 metres in 1984, it caused the IAAF to redesign the men's javelin (and later the women's, too) for safety purposes. The centre of gravity was brought forward, making it nose-dive into the ground sooner than before.

Ideal Physical Qualities

Athletes who excel in the Javelin are fast and dynamic, and good technique is more important than sheer strength. Traditionally, the event has been dominated by athletes from Scandinavian countries, with the Javelin pretty much being the national sport in Finland, for example.

Jan Zelezny

With Olympic titles from Atlanta 1996 and Sydney 2000, plus three world titles won between 1993 and 2001, Jan Zelezny is generally regarded as the greatest javelin thrower in history.

A long-time world record-holder, with a best of 98.48m, the Czech athlete also dominates the all-time global rankings.

Zelezny retired in 2006 with just one blemish on his career. He never won the European title, as he was always beaten by Britain's Steve Backley, who took the title from 1990 to 2002.

Clothing and Footwear

Javelin shoes look a little more like boots than other track and field footwear. The Javelin is a gruelling event, with the feet slamming on the ground as the athlete brakes hard during the final stages of the throw. So specialist shoes have lots of support and also spikes for grip.

As well as the standard singlet and shorts, javelin throwers also often use strapping or supports for the knees or their backs. It is also common to strap the feet and ankles to minimise movement within the shoes.

Fast with powerful upper bodies are the physical traits of successful Javelin throwers.

Lycra shorts and singlets are typically worn for this event and athletes often use strapping to support their knees, backs and ankles.

Specialist Javelin shoes have lots of support and spikes for extra grip.

Standards to aspire to

	Senior	U20	U17	U15	U13
Men	37.00m (800g)	37.00m (800g)	35.00m (700g)	30.00m (600g)	18.00m (400g)
Women	25.00m (600g)	25.00m (600g)	23.00m (600g)	18.00m (600g)	13.00m (400g)

The Javelin Throw is unique compared to other Throwing events, as athletes are not restricted by a small throwing circle. Allied to the aerodynamic qualities of the spear, this leads to some dazzling distances.

The Javelin

A javelin has three parts – a head, a shaft and a cord grip. The shaft can be solid or hollow, is made of metal or a similar material and is smooth. The metal head that is attached to the shaft has a sharp point, although children's javelins are also made with softer heads.

The grip covers the javelin's centre of gravity and does not exceed the diameter of the shaft by more than 8 millimetres. It has a smooth surface, but does not have any notches or indents.

Adult javelins are 800 grams for men and 600 grams for women, with the men's javelin 2.6–2.7 metres long and the women's 2.2–2.3m.

Personal implements can be used if they are passed by officials.

Arena Facts

Unlike other throws, which take place from a circle, the javelin is thrown from a runway. This runway is at least 30m long and the throw is made from behind an arc of a circle drawn with a radius of 8m. This arc is a 7-centimetre-wide white strip either painted or made of wood or plastic.

Javelin is one of the most physically taxing field events.

Throwing

Importantly, the javelin has to be held at the grip and thrown a certain way (see Key Rules below). Non-orthodox styles are not allowed.

During the throw itself, the attempt will only be valid if the tip of the metal head strikes the ground before any other part of the javelin – although it does not need to stick in. It must also land within the sector lines.

The number of attempts varies from three to six depending on the type of competition, and the measurement is taken from the point of landing nearest

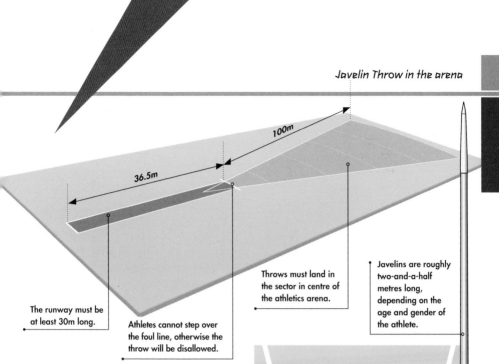

100m

36.5m

The runway must be at least 30m long.

Athletes cannot step over the foul line, otherwise the throw will be disallowed.

Throws must land in the sector in centre of the athletics arena.

Javelins are roughly two-and-a-half metres long, depending on the age and gender of the athlete.

the arc to the inner rim of the arc, and is recorded to the nearest centimetre below the reading unless the reading is an exact centimetre.

Safety

As the javelin can reach speeds of 95–110 kilometres per hour, extreme care should be taken when practising – or competing in – the Javelin, especially in wet conditions.

Athletes need to consider their own health, too, as it is one of the most physically taxing events on the entire Athletics programme.

Key Rules

- The javelin must be held at the grip and be thrown over the shoulder or upper part of the throwing arm.
- Throwers cannot turn their backs on the area the javelin has been thrown into during the attempt.

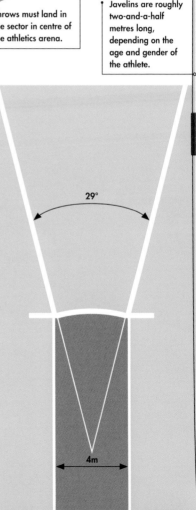

29°

4m

Javelin Throw techniques explained

Javelin throwers run quickly toward the throwing zone and then stop sharply, unleashing the spear with a cracking action. If executed properly, the javelin will fly to a tremendous distance.

Holding the Javelin

When it comes to gripping the javelin, there are three main methods. The American grip uses the thumb and index finger holding the back of the cord. The Finnish method sees the thumb and middle finger hold the cord with the index finger. The Fork grip sees the javelin held between the middle and index fingers.

One way to find a natural grip is to stick the javelin point in the ground and then slide your hand down so that the index or second finger is to the rear of the binding; the javelin should lie along the gap formed from the middle of the base of the hand to the division between the thumb and index finger.

Technique

The distance achieved in the Javelin is due to three main factors: speed, angle and height of release. The run-up can be anywhere from half a dozen to 20 steps (fewer steps for beginners) and

American grip

Fork grip

Finnish grip

The run-up can be anywhere from 12-20 steps and is undertaken on the balls of the feet.

The body remains sideways as the athlete moves. The throwing arm keeps parallel to the ground.

The 'soft step' prepares the thrower for the final stage of the throw.

is undertaken on the balls of the feet with the body slightly sideways to the direction of the throw and the throwing arm held higher than shoulder height.

The athlete's feet should be in line with the throwing direction and the hips kept forward. The throwing arm, meanwhile, is held parallel to the ground. It should be long and relaxed, with the palm pointing upward.

A crucial part comes before the throw when the right foot hits the ground and the right knee bends (if the thrower is right-handed). This is called the soft step and, if properly executed, prepares the athlete for the final stage of the throw.

As this soft step happens, the body continues moving forward at speed and the left arm extends to point towards the direction of the throw. The weight passes over the right foot during this stage and the left foot hits the ground with a bracing action. In short, the rear leg drives the hips to the front, transferring the weight from right to left leg.

Imagine the body acting as a drawn bow: as the left side of the body braces itself, the right hip will rotate forward, followed by the ribs and chest coming forward. All this time, the throwing arm stays back for as long as possible and then, finally, as the shoulder is whipped over the body, the throwing arm follows.

The elbow bends slightly, similar to a tennis serve, but then straightens and, lastly, follows through after the javelin is released over the athlete's head at an angle of about 30–35 degrees to the ground. The amount of space required to stop is usually about 2 metres and checkmarks are often used.

Technique Tips
- Increase your speed during the run-up.
- Lean backward slightly during the run-up and keep the hips forward.
- Ensure you brace your left-hand side (if you are right-handed) firmly as you prepare to throw.

Similar to a tennis serve, the javelin is finally released. Try to follow through at a 30–35 degree angle for a good distance.

As the soft step happens, the body weight passes over the stepping foot and the other foot hits the ground in a bracing action.

The amount of space required to stop is usually 2 metres.

Javelin Throw training techniques

Time spent with a javelin in the hand is good, but you will also benefit from doing lots of work without a javelin. Throwing other objects, bounding and flexibility exercises, for example, are all important.

In training, relatively equal time should be spent working on technique, flexibility and power. Drills to improve these areas include:

Medicine Ball Throw

These will help you shift your centre of gravity and channel power from the legs to the arms.

For a standing medicine ball throw, bend your knees, arc your back and throw the ball with hands above your head in a similar style to a football throw-in action.

Another good drill is to kneel down on both knees, or sit on the floor with legs out in front of you, and throw the ball with both hands above your head to a partner or against a wall.

Another twist on these exercises is to throw at targets, using a baseball, tennis or cricket ball.

Finally, progress to a three-step medicine ball throw, with a fast final left–right landing, and then try this three-step throw with a javelin.

Flexibility

This is very important in the Javelin and lots of attention should be paid to making your elbows, shoulders, back and ankles as mobile – and also as strong – as possible.

One simple but useful and specific stretch is to stand opposite a wall holding a javelin as you would just before throwing. Let the tip of the javelin touch the wall and, with weight on your left foot and pointing your right leg back slightly, let your arm extend upward and backward (stretching the shoulders) and push your hips forward.

Power and strength

Practise throwing a variety of heavy objects. In the weights room, the pull-over is a useful exercise. Plate twists with a heavy disc or weight held in both hands are another good exercise.

Plyometrics are also very important in building leg strength (see page 46). Depth jumping is particularly appropriate.

A general all-round weights programme and circuit training during the off-season period are great, too.

Training Tips

- Practise holding the javelin as much as possible during drills and running exercises in order for it to feel more natural in your hand.
- Use heavier medicine balls and weighted javelins to promote leg strength and action, while lighter implements help arm and shoulder movements.

- Ropes, pulleys or elastic cords can be used to hold back the throwing arm while encouraging the hips forward.

Common Faults and Remedies

- If you run up too fast and cannot adopt a good throwing position, then slow down and practise walking throws and then three- and five-stride run-ups.
- When the point of the javelin is not in line with the direction of the throw, keep the javelin on the palm of your hand with the fingers pointing to the rear. During the final stage of the throw, point your left hand in the direction of the throw.
  - If the arm is used too soon, wait for your front foot to land first.

Throwing other objects, bounding and flexibility exercises will all contribute to strong throws.

The big day

When you have fine-tuned
your technique, worked on
your speed and strength and
improved your flexibility as
much as you can, the next
stage is to put it all together
on competition day itself.

Your first event

Early competitions will always be nerve-racking for a rookie athlete, but following this simple guide will make the process easier. Pre-event preparation is essential if you are going to make the most of your potential.

If you have followed the advice in this book, you will already be a member of a club and have an experienced coach to guide you. If so, finding competitions will not be difficult. If you are struggling to find events, then look for fixtures listed in magazines such as *Athletics Weekly* or on websites like uka.org.uk.

Most athletes start by competing against athletes their own age in their own town, city or county. If good enough, they will progress to regional competitions, national events and, finally international meetings.

Nutrition

A good pre-event meal is vital. This should mainly consist of easily digestible carbohydrates, with a small amount of protein, and be eaten about 90 minutes to three hours before you compete.

Ensure you are well hydrated, too, but drink plenty over the previous 24 hours as opposed to the final hour before the competition, otherwise you will be needing constant toilet breaks as you head out into the athletics arena.

Warm-up

Depending on the weather, you will first need to make sure your body temperature is warm. Start slowly with walking and jogging and then move on to more dynamic stretches and strides. Finally, do some event-specific warm-up exercises – some practice jumps or throws, for example, if there is a suitable area outside the main arena.

Pre-event routine

After your pre-event meal, eaten a 90 minutes to three hours before the competition, it is good to sit down in order to relax and focus your mind before beginning your warm-up routine maybe an hour before the competition begins.

All athletes develop their own routines – realising what works and what does not – but the essentials are to make sure you are properly warmed up physically, fresh and focused mentally, and full of energy from a good pre-event meal that has been properly digested.

Finally, good luck! You are ready to jump or throw a personal best performance! And perhaps the Olympic Games itself will beckon one day…

Mental Preparation

Visualising how you are going to do in the competition is a useful exercise. Picturing yourself successfully moving through each stage of your jump or throw can give you confidence. Try to set some time aside to do this in a quiet, relaxed place.

You are on Your Own ... Almost

Once in the competition environment, you stand or fall by your own efforts, but it is still possible to glance into the stands to get the occasional thumbs up from your coach. If coaches are at competitions, they can watch and deliver vital advice after the event. Linked to this, do not get distracted by friends and family watching you. Use their cheers, but do not lose your focus.

Useful Items to Remember

- Safety pins – in order to attach your competition number to your vest.
- Vaseline or chalk – anti-chafing substances or something to improve your grip might be needed, depending on your event.
- Tape – this can be used to mark out checkpoints on the runway.
- Water bottle – don't get dehydrated if the competition is longer than you expect. Always have a drink to hand.

Committing to organised competitions is a fantastic means of measuring your progress.

Index

Picture credits

The publishers would like to thank the following sources for their kind permission to reproduce the pictures in this book.

Action Images: /Kim Kyung-Hoon/Reuters: 8-9, 108; /Dylan Martinez/Reuters: 78; /Jason O'Brien: 54; /Kai Pfaffenbach/Reuters: 11, 25, 34, 105, 116; /Wolfgang Rattay/Reuters: 63; /Ian Waldie/Reuters: 80

Getty Images: /AFP: 18, 59, 73, 121, 123; /Gabriel Bouys/AFP: 29, 33, 47, 125; /Clive Brunskill: 20-21; /Simon Bruty: 114; /Central Press: 98; /Mark Dadswell: 31, 69; /Adrian Dennis/AFP: 6, 49, 90; /Darren England: 5; /Stu Forster: 23, 82; /Valery Hache/AFP: 45; /Alexander Hassenstein/Bongarts: 15, 39, 93; /Harry How: 89; /Andy Lyons: 52; /Mike Powell: 71; /Peter Read Miller/Time & Life Pictures: 106; /Rolls Press/Popperfoto: 12, 14; /Jewel Samad/AFP: 51; /Javier Soriano/AFP: 60; /Cameron Spencer: 41, /Michael Steele: 37, 46, 96, 113; /Bob Thomas/Popperfoto: 13

Press Association Images: /Arne Jonsson/Scanpix: 100

Every effort has been made to acknowledge correctly and contact the source and/or copyright holder of each picture and Carlton Books Limited apologises for any unintentional errors or omissions that will be corrected in future editions of this book.